BARRON'S

A POCKET  GUIDE TO

Clichés

"Hit the Road"

Arthur Bell
Professor of Management Communication
McLaren School of Business
University of San Francisco

W9-ATL-506

Barron's Educational Series, Inc.

Dedication

To my children, Art, Lauren,
and Madeleine—true originals

© Copyright 1999 by Barron's Educational Series, Inc.

All inquiries should be addressed to:
Barron's Educational Series, Inc.
250 Wireless Boulevard
Hauppauge, NY 11788
http://www.barronseduc.com

Library of Congress Catalog Card No. 98-21311

International Standard Book No. 0-7641-0672-4

Library of Congress Cataloging-in-Publication Data
Bell, Arthur H. (Arthur Henry), 1946–
    A pocket guide to clichés / Arthur H. Bell.
        p.   cm.
    ISBN 0-7641-0672-4
    1. English language—Terms and phrases—Dictionaries.
2. English language—Usage—Dictionaries.   3. Clichés—
Dictionaries.   4. Figures of speech.   I. Title.
PE1689.B45   1998
423'.1—dc21   98-21311
                                                             CIP

PRINTED IN THE UNITED STATES OF AMERICA
9 8 7 6 5 4 3 2

Introduction

A cliché is a word or expression that gained popularity for cleverness or aptness of expression. Its popularity, unfortunately, was also its curse. As a cliché came into wider and wider use over a period of time, it lost its freshness of expression and became—well, a cliché. Expressions that make no attempt at such cleverness or aptness may gain widespread usage but are not true clichés. For example, *the shoe is on the other foot* is a cliché; *a sigh of relief* is merely a common descriptive expression.

This is not to say that clichés die out when they become stale. The clichés collected here are all alive and well in American English, both in conversation and in the full range of writing from short stories to articles to business documents. Because clichés form an integral and enduring part of the fabric of spoken and written English, they need definition and exemplification for at least three audiences:

- native speakers of American English, who may know the clichés of their own generation but not those of other generations. Many college students at present, for example, do not understand older clichés such as *on the fritz* or *pet peeves*. The same point can be made of regional differences in understanding.

- nonnative speakers of American English, who cannot look up clichés in standard dictionaries and, heaven knows, cannot understand them by literal interpretation. (Imagine a nonnative speaker's difficulty in using the literal meaning of *whole ball of wax* or *get the ax* in trying to understand those phrases.)

- writers and speakers who want to sensitize themselves to clichés, perhaps with the goal of avoiding them when original expression is called for or using them with skill when it proves advantageous to ring familiar bells (to use a cliché) with an audience. That latter use has been of particular importance for politicians, businesspeople, teachers, and entertainers, all of whom use clichés often to establish rapport (*break the ice*) and simplify or crystallize concepts (*cut to the chase*) for their readers or listeners.

Alphabetizing is the library style of word by word (something follows nothing), rather than letter by letter. For example, *not worth a plugged nickel* comes before *note of concern*, and *once in a blue moon* follows *on the warpath*. Parenthetical insertions are not considered in alphabetizing. A hyphen is treated as a space, but an apostrophe is not.

This collection of common expressions and clichés is by no means exhaustive. The author and publishers welcome reader suggestions for additional entries if and when a new edition of this work appears. These suggestions, or other comments, can be sent directly to the author by E-mail at bell@usfca.edu, or by regular mail: Professor Arthur Bell, McLaren School of Business, University of San Francisco, 2130 Fulton St., San Francisco, CA 94920.

Acknowledgments

This collection of clichés was compiled with helpful contributions from the following:
- my MBA and Executive MBA students at the McLaren School of Business, University of San Francisco;
- managers of Deutsche Telekom, Nippon Telegraph and Telephone, China Resources, Guangdong Enterprises, and British Telecommunications, all of whom helped me locate clichés that prove especially opaque for nonnative speakers of American English;
- and American managers and executives at Citibank, Sun Microsystems, Cost Plus World Markets, American Stores, Charles Schwab, PaineWebber, and the U.S. State Department, who kept track of clichés they encountered most often in their professional lives.

To all, I am sincerely grateful.

Thanks also go to Dean Gary Williams, Associate Deans Denis Neilson and Eugene Muscat, and my faculty colleagues at the McLaren School of Business for their interest in and support of this project.

My family, as always, has been my mainstay during the inevitable writing weekends that postponed other activities.

Finally, I'm deeply grateful to Grace Freedson, Max Reed, and the rest of the editorial and production team at Barron's Educational Series for their expert guidance and hard work on this project.

CLICHES

A

absence makes the heart grow fonder
The more we are apart from a person, the more we
yearn for his or her company.
> *John waved good-bye to Linda without much sorrow
> because he believed that* absence makes the heart grow
> fonder.

ace in the hole
A powerful resource saved to rescue a situation.
> *Because his mother was CEO of the company, Jack felt he
> had an* ace in the hole *for job security.*

actions speak louder than words
What a person does is more meaningful than what a
person says.
> *The boy did not trust the bully's apology because* actions
> speak louder than words.

add insult to injury
To follow an action that has caused harm by another
action that then offends the injured party.
> *The speeding ticket Wilson received after his accident* added
> insult to injury.

against the grain
To go in a direction opposite to the prevailing direction.
> *Campaigning for liberal candidates in the conservative
> area was going* against the grain *of the community.*

age before beauty
Honor or preference to a person's age is placed before
a person's physical attractiveness.
> *He held the door open for his older brother and joked about*
> age before beauty.

ahead of the game
At an advanced and advantageous position in comparison to expected or usual circumstances.
> *Having almost instant access to stock prices put the broker* *ahead of the game* *in managing her clients' assets.*

air one's dirty linen
To reveal negative or shameful information about oneself or one's associates.
> *The coach warned the team not to* *air their dirty linen* *to the press.*

albatross around one's neck
Perpetually burdened by misfortune.
> *The college degree she had purchased from a fly-by-night university proved to be an* *albatross around her neck* *for professional purposes.*

all ears
Listening closely.
> *The children were* *all ears* *when their parents began to speculate about getting a pet.*

all in a day's work
A performance that is not out of the ordinary.
> *Driving two hours to and from the job site was* *all in a day's work.*

all over but the shouting
The action has ended but the reaction continues.
> *When the basketball score reached 80 to 56, we knew it was* *all over but the shouting.*

all roads lead to Rome
All alternatives produce the same end result.
> *In discussing the different approaches to selling, the speaker made the point that* *all roads lead to Rome.*

all things to all men
Attempting, usually futilely, to fulfill many different expectations.

The new employee made the mistake of trying to be all things to all men.

all work and no play
Devoting too much energy to work activities and too little to recreational activities.

Most successful executives have been guilty at some time of all work and no play.

almighty dollar
The sole focus is on the importance of money.

We tired of his ceaseless worship of the almighty dollar.

ante up
To put up a tangible or financial sign of one's commitment.

The politician asked her supporters to ante up so that television ads could be purchased.

(the) apple doesn't fall far from the tree
One's personal characteristics can be attributed to one's parentage.

When the son was indicted along with the father, the whole community gossiped that the apple doesn't fall far from the tree.

apple of one's eye
One's favorite.

Harold loved all his children, but Jill was the apple of his eye.

armed to the teeth
Equipped far beyond the usual level with weapons.

The survivalist was armed to the teeth as he guarded his remote cabin.

arms of Morpheus
Asleep.
> *The long lecture caused students to drift into the arms of Morpheus.*

artsy-craftsy
Characterized by the more whimsical attitudes or skills of the artist or craftsman as opposed to those of the scientist.
> *He found the camp experience too artsy-craftsy for his taste.*

as hard as nails
Extremely difficult; unforgiving.
> *The new boss had a well-deserved reputation for being as hard as nails.*

as the crow flies
In a straight line between two points.
> *The distance was about five miles as the crow flies.*

asleep at the switch
Not alert in the area of one's responsibilities.
> *Someone was asleep at the switch when bills were mailed twice to the same customers.*

at a snail's pace
Very slowly.
> *The hand counting of ballots proceeded at a snail's pace compared to computer processing of the votes.*

at arm's length
Held at a distance in terms of relationship, influence, or association.
> *The bank president kept her nephew at arm's length during his first six months as an employee in her company.*

at each other's throats
In active and bitter conflict with one another.
> *The old political enemies were* at each other's throats *until they died.*

at face value
As a thing appears on the surface, not as it may be valued at a deeper level.
> *We took* at face value *her claim that she was once an actor.*

at first blush
Upon one's initial contact with or reaction to.
> At first blush, *the employee thought her supervisor was unreasonable in his demands.*

at loose ends
With no fixed or organized plan or purpose.
> *After a hectic semester, the students felt* at loose ends *during their vacation period.*

at sixes and sevens
At a point of indecision or confusion.
> *The manager was* at sixes and sevens *over whom to hire for the new position.*

at the drop of a hat
Quickly; with little notice.
> *Always impulsive by nature, he would fly to Europe* at the drop of a hat *to meet friends.*

at (one's) wit's end
At a point of ultimate frustration.
> *The harried teacher was* at her wit's end *with the unruly youngsters.*

average Joe

A person (usually male) of unremarkable characteristics, typical of those possessed by the vast middle portion of a population.

Although rumored to be smart and rich, Alex turned out to be just your average Joe.

avoid like the plague

To stay away from, as if from a life-threatening disease.

He vowed to avoid like the plague any job that required air travel.

ax to grind

A problem to air or issue to dispute.

The persistent reporter apparently had an ax to grind with the candidate.

B

babe in the woods
An innocent, inexperienced person.
Fresh from high school, the new pitcher was a babe in the woods compared to the veteran players who made up the rest of the big league team.

(on the) back burner
Not urgent; positioned for later action or attention.
We assured the school board that the proposal could be placed on the back burner until the members had time to consider it thoroughly.

back to square one
To give up all progress and return to where one began.
The rocket explosion took the space program back to square one.

back to the salt mines
To return to undesirable tasks; often said of work life.
After a long lunch, the workers joked that it was time to go back to the salt mines.

backseat driver
One who is not positioned to be in control but who nevertheless gives advice to those who are.
Although he knew little about home design, he was glad to be a backseat driver to the architect hired to create blueprints for the project.

bag and baggage
With all of one's possessions; entirely.
We were appalled when our eight distant relatives arrived bag and baggage at our door.

bald-faced lie
An untruth presented without disguise.
His claim to be a former opera singer is a bald-faced lie.

(how the) ball bounces
With the randomness and purposelessness of chance experience.
We hated to see the outdoor picnic rained out, but that's how the ball bounces.

ball is in one's court
Responsibility for action or response has been given over to one party from another.
During the negotiations, the ambassador told the foreign leader that the ball was in his court.

ball of fire
A source, usually a person, characterized by a high level of seemingly inexhaustible energy.
The veteran chef was a ball of fire when it came to preparing holiday meals for the homeless.

ballpark estimate
An approximation.
Remodeling will cost $20,000, as a ballpark estimate.

bang for the buck
Value received for money (or something else) invested.
Military leaders wanted to get as much bang for the buck as possible from their expenditures on new weapons systems.

bang-up job
Excellent, praiseworthy performance or achievement.
The students did a bang-up job in decorating the gymnasium for the spring dance.

baptism by fire
A challenging, often painful initiation into a new experience, life stage, or membership.
Joining the running team without first getting in shape proved to be a baptism by fire.

bark is worse than one's bite
One's verbal threats or protestations are far in excess
of one's actions.

*Although gruff at times, the boss was one of those people
whose bark is worse than their bite.*

bark up the wrong tree
To pursue a search for clues or answers in the wrong
direction.

*Investigators began to bark up the wrong tree when they
believed the convict's imaginative alibi.*

basket case
A situation or person characterized by almost complete
disorientation, disorganization, or emotional upset.

*After weeks of personal and professional stress, Linda was
a basket case.*

bat out of hell
Moving with frantic speed.

He bolted from the starting line like a bat out of hell.

bated breath
With suspense, as in holding one's breath.

*We waited with bated breath to see if the hot air balloon
would clear the high-tension electric wires.*

battle of nerves
Tense interpersonal conflict or confrontation carried
on at an emotional or intellectual level rather than a
physical level.

*The chess champions braced themselves for a prolonged
battle of nerves.*

be a fly on the wall
To be an unseen observer.

*I would like to be a fly on the wall when she opens
the present.*

bean counter
A person, often said of accountants, who pays attention to minute and often trivial items within a larger circumstance or experience.

The hiring committee resolved not to employ a bean counter to lead the New Products division.

beat around the bush
To speak or act in ways that are irrelevant to the main issue.

In a one-minute TV ad, the candidate had no time to beat around the bush.

beat the drum for
To speak or act with enthusiasm on behalf of.

It was not difficult to find friends to beat the drum for Ellen's nomination.

beat to the punch
To take action before receiving the impact of a similar or related action.

One development team wanted to beat the other to the punch in delivering a prototype of the new product.

beating a dead horse
Continuing to advocate a lost or hopeless cause or issue.

Continuing to rehash political arguments from the 1980s was beating a dead horse.

beauty sleep
Rest or sleep taken to perpetuate one's physical attractiveness; often said humorously.

She retired early with the explanation that she needed her beauty sleep.

bed of roses
A soft, fragrant place of repose.

Camping our way across Africa was hardly a bed of roses.

beef (something) up
To increase size, strength, durability, or influence.
The boat designer decided to beef up the hull.

behind the eight ball
Not positioned advantageously in a game, process, or competition.
Entering school in the third week put Jackson behind the eight ball in most of his classes.

(to go) belly up
To go bankrupt; to fail.
The company went belly up after losing its three main clients.

belt it out
To sing or speak with physical gusto.
The crowd cheered as the singer began to belt out the national anthem.

bend over backwards
To make extraordinary, even self-sacrificing, efforts to accommodate someone else's will or preferences.
The service representative pledged to bend over backwards to please customers.

bent out of shape
Angry, or otherwise distorted from one's usual emotional state.
We were surprised that such a trivial incident would cause him to be bent out of shape.

best foot forward
To make one's most advantageous attributes or appearances visible or prominent before less advantageous aspects.
Her advice to me was to put my best foot forward in job interviews.

best thing since sliced bread
A revolutionary new development or advancement; usually said with purposeful exaggeration.
The on/off switch for the telephone seemed like the best thing since sliced bread.

better late than never
It is preferable to deliver or perform later than expected rather than not at all.
Cliff explained that his career as a jazz pianist came better late than never.

between a rock and a hard place
Faced with two equally undesirable choices or realities.
The washed-out bridge and the tree-strewn highway left the travelers between a rock and a hard place.

between the devil and the deep blue sea
Faced with two dangerous but somewhat seductive choices or realities.
In deciding whether to attend the party with Tom or Lance, Wendy felt she was choosing between the devil and the deep blue sea.

between the lines
Finding the message hidden at a deeper level beneath the surface of spoken or written words.
Reading between the lines, I felt that the company's letter communicated a patronizing attitude toward its clientele.

beyond a doubt
Indisputable.
Her friends are beyond a doubt the most unusual group of people I have ever met.

beyond the pale
Outside the farthest boundaries of taste, belief, or convention.
Serving champagne at the church luncheon was beyond the pale for many congregation members.

big frog in a small pond
A person whose importance is large due only to the small environment in which he or she exists.

Although the professor at the little-known college had written six books, she was actually a big frog in a small pond.

big league
At the highest levels; of the utmost quality, skill, or expertise.

To solve our company's financial woes, we need a big-league consultant.

big picture
The view that provides full context and perspective.

The news commentator failed to see the big picture in criticizing the tax reduction measure.

big shoes to fill
When previous roles or activities were performed so well as to be intimidating to the next person who attempts those roles or activities.

When its Oscar-winning producer retired, the studio had big shoes to fill in finding her replacement.

big-time spender
One who spends extravagantly and ostentatiously.

Uncle Evan turned into a big-time spender whenever he visited Las Vegas.

birds of a feather flock together
Those with similar interests and attributes tend to seek and keep one another's company.

When the two psychiatrists married one another, their friends joked that birds of a feather flock together.

bite off more than one can chew
To take on tasks or responsibilities that are beyond one's ability to fulfill.

Taking more than four classes per semester may be biting off more than you can chew.

bite the bullet
To brace oneself to endure pain or hardship in order to survive or directly confront a challenge or threat.
Rather than pay more for repairs, the superintendent decided to bite the bullet *and replace the air-conditioning system entirely.*

bite the dust
To die; to come to a less-than-heroic end.
We suspected that the hero of the cowboy movie would bite the dust *in the end.*

bite the hand that feeds you
To reject, often spitefully, the help of a benefactor.
When they complained about government procedures, the manager warned the salespeople not to bite the hand that feeds them.

black sheep
Ostracized group member who breaks conventions and taboos.
Two years in a reform school branded Jim as the black sheep *of the family.*

blank check
A commitment without specified limits.
As an expression of her confidence in us, the director assured us of a blank check *in making hotel and travel arrangements.*

blaze a trail
To create new access in such a way that it can be useful for others; to be a front-runner.
The astronaut blazed a trail *for all others to follow.*

(down a) blind alley
A direction of pursuit that leads nowhere.
Looking for clues among her personal possessions was going down a blind alley.

blind leading the blind
Those without insight are in the undesirable role of showing the way to others who are also without insight.
The idea of asking new managers to lead training seminars for other managers is a case of the blind leading the blind.

blood in the eye
Empassioned or angry to an extreme degree.
He faced his accusers with blood in his eye.

blood is thicker than water
One is bound more deeply to one's relatives than to others.
We were surprised when Jeff resigned to join his parents' company, but blood is thicker than water.

blow it
To make a significant and often irremediable mistake; to lose an advantage.
The team had an early lead in the game and didn't want to blow it.

blow one's cover
To reveal one's true identity after attempting to hide it.
The spy wore a wig in an effort not to blow her cover.

blow one's own horn
To boast about oneself and one's achievements or abilities.
The prize winner felt that making any kind of speech at the awards ceremony would be blowing her own horn.

blow one's stack
To exhibit sudden, explosive anger.
The news of severe financial losses in the last quarter will cause the boss to blow his stack.

blow smoke
To communicate in a way that tends to hide the truth or disguise one's ignorance.
Some of the students were blowing smoke in their attempts to complete the difficult essay question.

blow the whistle on
To report the misdeeds of someone.
For the sake of public safety, sometimes an employee must blow the whistle on his or her own company.

blue in the face
To the limits of physical and emotional effort.
We argued with him until we were blue in the face, but to no avail.

bogged down
Slowed almost to the stopping point.
The committee became bogged down in disagreements over procedures.

boggle the mind
To have an encounter so surprising or outrageous as to throw the mind into confusion, amazement, or awe.
Two theories of an expanding universe boggle the mind.

boils down to
To arrive at the final meaning or essence after surface or unimportant aspects have been eliminated.
The entire proposition boils down to a simple moral choice.

bolt from the blue
Sudden, lightninglike occurrence or inspiration.
The announcement of her accomplishment came like a bolt from the blue.

bone of contention
Issue over which there is significant disagreement.
Exactly which prescription drugs the health plan would pay for remained a bone of contention.

bone to pick
A disputed issue to raise.
The coach had a bone to pick with the referee who had called the foul.

bored silly
Extremely uninterested to the point of giddiness.
Most of the students appeared to be bored silly by the video-taped lecture.

born with a silver spoon (in one's mouth)
Given advantages of wealth or position from an early age.
With a large trust fund in her name, Mary could rightly be said to be born with a silver spoon in her mouth.

bottom dollar
Last of the money one possesses.
We spent our bottom dollar for the home we wanted.

bottom fishing
Attempting to capture less desirable objects or goals in less-than-ideal locations.
Probably the company should pay more for a qualified employee instead of bottom fishing for someone who will work for less.

bottomless pit
A receptacle with seemingly limitless capacity.
The couple joked that their youngest daughter was a bottomless pit at a restaurant.

brain drain
Relocation over time of the brightest minds.
Many less-developed countries experience a brain drain as their citizens study abroad, then never return.

brave the elements
To endure inclement weather.
Part of basic training was learning to brave the elements without becoming ill.

bread and butter
One's main source of sustenance or financial gain.
> *Poor workmanship by the original builders was the carpenter's bread and butter.*

break the ice
To initially attempt to achieve social rapport.
> *The first awkward moments at the party were spent in unsuccessful efforts to break the ice.*

breakneck pace
A speed so extreme as to approach the point of danger.
> *To prepare for the Christmas holidays, production line employees worked at a breakneck pace.*

breathe down one's neck
To supervise, oversee, or pursue a person in such a close way as to cause feelings of discomfort and resentment.
> *Frank didn't mind his supervisor's suggestions, but he did resent having someone breathe down his neck all day.*

breathe fire
To express oneself with extreme anger or hostility.
> *The previous dean would virtually breathe fire when faculty members requested smaller classes.*

breathing room
Sufficient emotional or physical distance, in time or space, to regain one's bearings and energy.
> *Telecommuting two days a week gave Sam the breathing room he needed to be a good employee as well as a single parent.*

bring home the bacon
To get paid; achieve a financial goal.
> *She was eager to call on the new client and vowed to bring home the bacon.*

brings it home
Makes something real in familiar terms.
Reading about war leaves strong impressions, but talking to war veterans truly brings it home.

bright-eyed and bushy-tailed
Wide awake and full of energy.
The volunteers arrived bright-eyed and bushy-tailed at 7 A.M. to begin work on the project.

brush up on
To refresh one's knowledge or skills.
He decided to brush up on calculus before studying trigonometry.

build a better mousetrap
To invent a more effective solution to a common problem.
The CEO urged us not to worry about price wars with competitors but instead to put our energy into building a better mousetrap.

build a fire under
To motivate, with the suggestion of implied fear or pain.
Many citizens wanted to build a fire under the new police chief to take action after the rash of burglaries.

bull in a china shop
An unpredictable, destructive influence in a fragile environment.
The union organizer proved to be a bull in a china shop at the company picnic.

bull session
A conversation where participants feel free to express opinions and stretch the truth freely.
The alumni enjoyed joining in a general bull session with the coach at the beginning and end of each season.

bum rap
An unwarranted charge.
Richard faced a bum rap when the police charged him with a crime committed by his twin brother.

burn a hole in one's pocket
To cause an almost irresistible desire to spend.
Unexpected cash always burned a hole in his pocket.

burn one's bridges
To destroy social and professional links to previous people and organizations.
Be careful not to burn your bridges when leaving one employer for a new job.

burn the candle at both ends
To spend one's energy at a level that proves depleting and self-destructive.
By working all day and going to school at night, Brenda felt she was burning the candle at both ends.

burn the midnight oil
To work well past the usual quitting time.
Tax accountants usually must burn the midnight oil in the weeks just before April 15.

burr under one's saddle
An irritant that continues to cause discomfort in some form.
The car's noisy exhaust system was a perpetual burr under his father's saddle.

bury one's head in the sand
To purposely ignore facts and sensations that one finds unpleasant.
It often proves more useful to face problems directly rather than bury one's head in the sand.

bury the hatchet
To cease hostility; make peaceful arrangements.
The two feuding families agreed to bury the hatchet.

bust a gut
To exert oneself to one's physical or emotional limits.
One reporter boasted he would bust a gut to get the first interview with the newly elected senator.

butterflies in one's stomach
Symptoms of anticipatory anxiety.
On opening night, every actor feels butterflies in the stomach.

buy a pig in a poke
To make a purchase or accept a proposition without examining it carefully.
We knew that by buying products by telephone, we risked buying a pig in a poke.

buy the farm
To die.
The young pilot knew he had to regain control of the plane or else buy the farm.

buy time
To take action that provides additional time for achieving a goal.
The union strike allowed the company to buy time to assess its total financial picture.

C

call a spade a spade
To speak in plain, unmistakable language.
In using the word "incompetent" on the performance evaluation, Barbara had decided to call a spade a spade.

call him on the carpet
To summon a person for disciplinary action or accusation.
After Bob's many mistakes, his boss reluctantly had to call him on the carpet.

call it a night
To conclude a period of work or social engagement.
It's been a great party, but now we have to call it a night.

call of nature
The urge for elimination.
The hikers took a break to answer the call of nature.

calm before the storm
A period of low stress or activity before a period of high stress or activity.
Their honeymoon proved to be the calm before the storm.

can't make heads or tails of
To be unable to discover any identifying or clarifying information about something.
We read the instruction manual but could not make heads or tails of the assembly directions.

can't see the forest for the trees
To fail to see the larger context of a situation or idea because one focuses too narrowly on individual details.
In focusing too narrowly on local issues, our politicians do not see the forest for the trees.

can't stand (tolerate)
Has no patience with; can't put up with.
I can't stand his arrogance.

cards stacked against one
When prevailing opinions, prejudices, or criteria are not in one's favor.
> *The cards are stacked against John for the job because he has so little experience.*

carry (or have) a chip on one's shoulder
To be especially sensitive to some issue to the point of striking out in anger or other strong emotion when the issue is mentioned.
> *One of the players still has a chip on her shoulder from the last game with the cross-city rivals.*

carry a torch
To continue to have deep, often hidden affection for another.
> *Even though he hasn't seen her in years, Robert still carries a torch for Maria.*

carry coals to Newcastle
To make unnecessary and sometimes foolish efforts to provide what already exists.
> *We could sell heating units in Panama, but that seems like carrying coals to Newcastle.*

carry the ball
To bear primary responsibility or leadership for.
> *As our newly elected club president, it's now your turn to carry the ball.*

cart before the horse
Reversal of the appropriate order of importance.
> *Buying gifts before we've even met our new niece is putting the cart before the horse.*

cast pearls before swine
To waste valuable contributions on those who do not or cannot appreciate them.
> *Unable to quell the noisy crowd, the lecturer left abruptly, vowing never again to cast pearls before swine.*

catch a wink; to catch forty winks
Fall asleep for a brief period.

Let me catch a wink *before taking my turn at night watch.*

catch off guard
To approach someone in an unexpected way or at an
unexpected time.

*The interviewer received frank answers from the candidate
by* catching her off guard.

catch–22
An illogical situation that cannot turn out well no matter which alternatives are pursued.

*Owing taxes but being unable to find work because of tax
liens is the ultimate* catch–22.

caught red-handed
Apprehended in the midst of criminal or unprofessional
activity.

Thanks to the surveillance camera, the thieves were caught
red-handed.

chalk it up to experience
To interpret an undesirable experience as necessary
learning.

*Signing a lease with the new renter without checking credit
references proved to be unwise, but the landlord* chalked it
up to experience.

checkered past
A history that contains a mixture of honorable and
less-than-honorable experiences.

It was revealed that the mayor had a checkered past *in
another city.*

(something to) chew on
Something to consider, usually in a ruminative way
over a period of time.

*Her comments about early childhood education gave the
parents* something to chew on.

chicken feed
Relatively worthless cost or compensation.
The contractor wanted the job but didn't want to work for chicken feed.

chicken out
To back away from an experience out of fear.
Two of the teenagers stood in line to ride on the roller coaster, but then chickened out at the last minute.

chicken with its head cut off
Describing frantic, short-lived flight or exertion with no purpose.
When he learned of the car fire, Jack ran around like a chicken with its head cut off.

child's play
An easy activity or experience.
Programming the VCR was hardly child's play.

chill out
To completely relax.
After her presentation to the board, Tina wisely decided to chill out for the rest of the afternoon.

chip in
To contribute a share toward.
We should all chip in to buy her a going-away present.

chip off the old block
A child with attributes similar to those of the parent's.
By beating his father's long-standing track record, Juan proved to be a chip off the old block.

circle the wagons
To position oneself and one's allies or associates defensively.
After the hostile article about the company appeared in the newspaper, the CEO told all employees to circle the wagons as far as the press was concerned.

circular file
Trash can; waste basket.
In a fit of rage, she threw the tabloid into the circular file.

classic case
Something that is used to exemplify or support a concept or proposition.
His disappearance was a classic case of escaping after a crime.

clay pigeon
A helpless victim with no power to avoid its own destruction.
No one wants to be a clay pigeon for Hilda's verbal abuse.

clean bill of health
A physician's or other professional's opinion showing no illnesses or problems.
The auditors gave the firm a clean bill of health.

clean his clock
To take severe aggressive action against.
Victor promised to clean Trent's clock if he stole fruit from the tree again.

clean one out
To exhaust one's financial resources.
The repair bills from the winter storms cleaned out our savings account.

clean slate
A fresh beginning, without a record of past events.
In spite of past problems, she agreed to give her secretary a clean slate.

clean-up batter
The most powerful and most reliable performer.
They brought in Donna as their clean-up batter on the presentation team.

clean up one's act
To remove unsavory or unethical aspects from one's performance.
Before applying to graduate school, Ralph should clean up his act and learn some self-discipline.

clear as mud
Impenetrably obscure.
The so-called expert's explanations were as clear as mud.

climb the ladder
To rise step by step in the organization.
Some employees are content not to spend much energy trying to climb the ladder.

clock is ticking
Time is passing toward an impending deadline.
The couple have waited for years to have children, but now the clock is ticking.

close only counts in horseshoes
A performance that almost reaches a defined goal is still a failure.
He came within five percent of making his quota, but the sales manager told him close only counts in horseshoes.

close shave
An encounter or experience that came dangerously close to producing undesirable results.
The two huge yachts passed within a few feet of one another—it was a close shave!

cloud nine
A state of euphoria, unfettered excitement, and happiness.
The lottery winner was on cloud nine.

coin a phrase
To invent a term or description.
We called the builder the "wizard of walls," to coin a phrase.

cold hands, warm heart
Physical signals of social aloofness, such as cold hands, mask the reality of good intentions.
It was obvious from her handshake that she was nervous, but cold hands, warm heart.

cold turkey
Action that is taken suddenly, without transition.
Mr. Liu quit smoking cold turkey when he returned to Beijing.

come a long way
To make significant progress.
Pet shows have come a long way since their first days in empty warehouses.

come apart at the seams
To fail at the very points intended to keep the structure, organization, situation, or person intact.
After the entire executive staff resigned, the company began to come apart at the seams.

come down off one's high horse
To stop the posturing of false pride.
We all wished the minister would come down off his high horse and relate more naturally to the congregation.

come full circle
To return to a beginning point.
They knew things had come full circle when Gwen returned to work as a doctor at the hospital where she was born.

come home to roost
Problems that return to cause difficulty for the person or organization that attempted to banish these problems.
In spite of his efforts to forget, the early problems with his parents would come home to roost in his later years.

come out in the wash
To eventually be revealed for what it is.
The details may still be vague, but I'm sure they will all come out in the wash.

come out on top
To win; surpass all others.
Few fans suspected that State University would come out on top.

come unglued
To disintegrate (often emotionally).
Stress from the storm seemed to cause the ship's captain to come unglued.

come up for air
To take a period of relaxation and reenergization after intense activity.
After working day and night preparing the proposal, the entire team needed to take a day to come up for air.

common ground
Beliefs, ideas, or commitments held jointly.
The politician urged the various factions in the audience to find common ground.

company man
An employee whose priorities and ethics are solely those of the firm.
The idea of resigning to start their own firm appealed to all the engineers except Frank, who was a company man through and through.

compare apples and oranges
To make inaccurate comparisons between unlike categories.
Equating the high temperatures in one state to the amount of rain in another is comparing apples and oranges.

compare notes
To share insights and records, with the goal of checking perceptions and accuracy.
Before leaving the convention, we compared notes on what we found most valuable.

cook one's goose
To speak or take action in ways that lead to one's ultimate downfall.
Marilyn's unannounced vacation cooked her goose with senior management.

(how the) cookie crumbles
How things turn out, whether we like it or not.
The venture failed, but that's how the cookie crumbles.

cool as a cucumber
Emotionally controlled, without signs of nervous stress.
Throughout his trial, the defendant remained as cool as a cucumber.

cool customer
A self-controlled, emotionally contained person (not necessarily a customer).
No matter what the pressures of his job, the customs official remained a cool customer.

cool one's heels
To spend time in jail; more generally, to be placed unwillingly in confinement or restraint.
The driver had two days to cool his heels in the county jail before being released on bail.

cool one's jets
To calm down, especially after a period of intense energy.
Five of the performers took time to cool their jets in Miami before continuing the whirlwind tour.

couch potato
One who exercises little and spends a great deal of time lounging.
Many writers turn out to be couch potatoes and watch TV all day.

count one's chickens before they're hatched
To rely on anticipated gains or other positive developments before they have materialized.
Buying a new house before selling the old one seemed to be counting one's chickens before they're hatched.

count to ten
To refrain from acting on the basis of strong emotion until a period of time has passed.
The next time the boss speaks harshly to you, count to ten before replying.

cover the waterfront
To include in one's consideration a broad range of germane aspects of a topic area.
Believe me, we've covered the waterfront in planning security for the senator's visit.

crack of dawn
At dawn's first light.
The hunters arose at the crack of dawn.

crack the whip
To motivate others by harsh measures.
Johnson had to crack the whip to get his employees to arrive on time.

crank something out
To produce something in a way that emphasizes speed and de-emphasizes quality.
We don't have time to research the topic thoroughly, but I'm sure we can crank something out by the deadline.

crapshoot
An option that involves a high degree of chance.
Whether the space station is ever hit by space debris is a crapshoot.

cream of the crop
The best of those available.
The selection interviewers only wanted to meet the cream of the crop from the graduating class.

cream puff
Someone who lacks strength and can be easily manipulated or conquered.
Wilson proved to be something of a cream puff in labor negotiations.

crocodile tears
False signs of sorrow or remorse.
He shed crocodile tears over his boss's forced retirement.

cross one's fingers
To hope for good luck.
Many of the horseracing fans crossed their fingers as the horses left the starting gate.

crunch time
Period necessitating intense, sustained work if deadlines are to be met.
The designers had played with several ideas, but now it was crunch time.

cry over spilled milk
To show regret over events that cannot be changed.
> *It made no sense to* cry over spilled milk *once the contract was awarded to another company.*

(one's) cup of tea
One's preferences.
> *Jogging may be good exercise, but it just wasn't her* cup of tea.

cut a swath
To make one's action or influence clearly visible or remarkable.
> *With her diamonds and Paris gown, she* cut quite a swath *at the opening night.*

cut and dried
Exact; beyond dispute; uncompromising.
> *No theories in astrophysics are actually as* cut and dried *as they appear in college textbooks.*

cut and run
To retreat suddenly, often with implication of cowardice, from a stressful situation or confrontation.
> *We feared that most of the volunteers would* cut and run *after the first negative polls appeared.*

cut off one's nose to spite one's face
To act against one local irritant in a way that has a negative impact on one's larger interests.
> *It seemed senseless to* cut off one's nose to spite one's face *by canceling the entire engagement over a squabble.*

cut teeth
To get initial experience.
> *The ocean swimmer* cut her teeth *as a competitor in YWCA swim meets.*

cut the mustard
To perform at an expected standard.
> *The rock musician feared he couldn't cut the mustard with true jazz musicians.*

cut to the bone
To eliminate all but the most vital or important parts.
> *The final budget reductions cut to the bone in the Human Resources division.*

cut to the quick
To speak or act in such a way as to cause intense pain to another.
> *She was cut to the quick by her neighbor's unthinking remark.*

cutting edge
The latest, most advanced techniques or developments.
> *The computer manufacturer promised cutting edge technology in every aspect of the new laptop computer.*

D

damned if you do, damned if you don't
No available option will lead to desirable results.

In choosing one used car over another, you're often damned if you do, damned if you don't.

dark horse
A competitor thought to be unlikely to win.

The candidate was certainly a dark horse in most polls.

dead as a doornail
Unmistakably dead.

They spotted a mouse in the corner, but it was dead as a doornail.

dead duck
A lost cause, or person branded for failure.

The whole project was a dead duck once Susan's transfer was announced.

dead ringer
An exact replica or look-alike, usually for a person.

One of the older employees was a dead ringer for John Wayne.

denizens of the deep
Mysterious deep-water sea creatures.

At the city aquarium we saw sharks and other denizens of the deep.

devil to pay
Penalties or other very undesirable results from actions taken.

There will be the devil to pay if Dad's car isn't returned in good condition.

diamond in the rough
Something precious hidden beneath an unattractive exterior.

The guide dog looked like a mutt but was in fact a diamond in the rough for his master.

die is cast
The course of future events is determined and unchangeable.

No matter how many changes we may want to make in our tax system, the die is cast for years to come.

die with one's boots on
To end one's life, or otherwise conclude, while in the midst of one's lifework.

Retirement had little attraction for Nathan, who planned to die with his boots on.

different strokes for different folks
People are not the same; hence their choices, interests, and habits are not the same.

His son's earring bothered George at first, but he finally reconciled himself to the fact that there are different strokes for different folks.

dig in one's heels
To become stubborn; resist others' attempts to bring change.

The last thing we want is for the sellers to dig in their heels over trivial issues.

dime a dozen
Inexpensive to the point of being almost meaningless in price; commonplace.

Well-trained secretaries used to be a dime a dozen.

dirt cheap
Extremely inexpensive.

Compared to surrounding properties, this lot is dirt cheap.

dish something out
To present something, usually verbally, in an unrestrained and often gossipy way.

He hated criticism, but he could certainly dish it out.

dish the dirt
To spread negative information through gossip about others.
She lost no opportunity to dish the dirt about her coworkers.

divide and conquer
To win over one's foes or obstacles by attacking parts rather than the whole.
Probably the best way to cover the entire region is to divide and conquer.

do a double take
To take a sudden, second look after the surprise of an initial impression.
We did a double take after seeing the movie star in ordinary street clothes.

do a number on someone
To act deceptively to someone's disadvantage; try to force.
I should have been more careful, but the salesperson did a number on me from the time I entered the showroom.

do-gooder
A person who does good deeds, but often in ways that appear self-serving, naive, or manipulative to others.
They wished the do-gooders had been more practical in their approach to aiding the storm-damaged neighborhood.

do one's (own) thing
To pursue one's own special interests.
The boss won't get our best work until he frees each of us to do our own thing.

do time
To serve a prison sentence.
The judge warned that Henderson would do time if arrested and convicted again.

doctor's orders
A physician's order to the patient; more generally, the instructions of an expert for the well-being of a project, organization, or individual.

The company president explained that layoffs were just following doctor's orders in returning the company to profitability.

dog and pony show
A presentation characterized by polished style, frequent use of visual aids, and high entertainment values.

At the trade show we expected to see a dog and pony show at almost every booth.

dog-eared pages
Pages that have the corners folded over, thus resembling dogs' ears.

The child's favorite book had dog-eared pages.

dog in the manger
One who acts to prevent others from receiving advantages that he or she cannot have.

Because he didn't receive the nomination, Irving played dog in the manger to anyone else seeking the office.

domino effect
The chain reaction that occurs when one event causes the next in an unstoppable series.

When the currency of one nation is devalued, a domino effect often ensues in the region.

dose of one's own medicine
Receiving the results of proposed solutions or other advice given to others.

The coach should take a dose of his own medicine when it comes to the importance of daily exercise.

dot the i's and cross the t's
To take excruciating care with every aspect of an undertaking.
We had to make sure to dot the "i's" and cross the "t's" on the negotiation before recommending the final contract for approval.

down at the heels
Visibly impoverished.
After six months without work, he looked and felt down at the heels.

down for the count
Impacted negatively to such a degree that recovery is impossible.
Without its Asian suppliers, the small company was down for the count.

down in the dumps
Melancholy; depressed.
Don't be down in the dumps over events you can't control.

down on one's luck
Experiencing a period of sustained misfortune.
Owen complained that he had been down on his luck ever since leaving Cincinnati.

down (or up) one's alley
In keeping with one's special areas of experience or skill.
That job opportunity is right down your alley.

down the hatch
Drinking a few single gulps with gusto.
With a hearty cry of "Down the hatch!" the crew members toasted their victory.

down the tubes

On an irreversible course to failure or destruction.

The travel plans went down the tubes after the hurricane turned south.

down to the wire

The success or accomplishment of an undertaking will not be known until the very last minute.

Even with overtime, the team's work on the report came down to the wire.

down with the ship

Describing a leader of an undertaking who is committed to personal downfall if the undertaking fails.

Part of becoming a senior manager in the firm will mean being willing to go down with the ship on projects assigned to you.

draw a bead on

To take precise aim at.

For career success, draw a bead on your most desired personal goals.

draw a blank

To search for an item of information but fail to find it.

I tried to remember his name, but I drew a blank.

dressed to kill

Clothed with an eye toward maximum desired impact on others.

She stepped from the limousine dressed to kill.

dressed to the nines

Clothed in the height of fashion.

He was dressed to the nines for the exhibition of ballroom dancing.

drink like a fish

To consume an excessive amount of alcohol.

Jack would be more pleasant if he didn't drink like a fish.

drop-dead date
The date after which no further extensions can be granted.
> *The editor expected the manuscript by April 1, but April 6 was actually the drop-dead date.*

drop in the bucket
An extremely small contribution to an immense need.
> *His donation, unfortunately, was only a drop in the bucket when it came to the organization's true financial needs.*

drop the ball
To fail in one's duties or responsibilities.
> *We hoped Larry wouldn't drop the ball again in arranging tours for our international guests.*

drown one's sorrows
To drink as a way of putting one's problems out of mind.
> *It wasn't a good habit for the sales group to drown their sorrows each time they lost a client.*

drunk as a skunk
Extremely inebriated.
> *Allen appeared quiet and pale, but he was in fact drunk as a skunk.*

(not) dry behind the ears
Still in a newborn state; inexperienced.
> *Most of the new recruits didn't seem dry behind the ears.*

dry run
A test that does not involve full deployment of operational resources.
> *Let's schedule a dry run before putting the unit into full production.*

duck soup
Something that is very easy.
> *This assignment turned out to be duck soup.*

(get one's) ducks in a row
To organize an undertaking under one's control.
Before discussing company reorganization, let's make sure we have our present ducks in a row.

dutch treat
Payment shared equally by participants in a social event.
They felt most comfortable making their first date a dutch treat.

Dutch uncle
A person (usually older) who gives advice, often unasked for.
Pardon me for sounding like a Dutch uncle, but you really should check with your lawyer first.

E

eager beaver

A person with boundless enthusiasm.

We need more eager beavers like Xavier on our squad.

eagle eye

One who watches developments closely and carefully.

You can trust an executive like Ramirez as the eagle eye for approaching storms.

ear to the ground

Listening for signs of future developments and events.

The rumors probably aren't true, but keep your ear to the ground nonetheless.

early bird gets the worm

The person who acts early in a competitive situation has a better chance of receiving the reward.

The early bird gets the worm, especially when it comes to flea market shopping.

earn one's stripes

To perform in ways that qualify one for organizational or public recognition.

He earned his stripes as an airline pilot before starting his own air commuting business.

easier said than done

A task is easier to talk about than to do.

Staying focused on long-term goals is easier said than done.

(as) easy as 1, 2, 3

A task is as easy to accomplish as counting.

Learning to ski with Hans was as easy as 1, 2, 3.

easy come, easy go

Something that comes to us easily can also leave us just as easily.

We won $100 during our first night in Las Vegas, but easy come, easy go.

eat like a bird
To eat very little.
The child ate like a bird, but the pediatrician told the parents not to be concerned.

eat like a horse
To eat constantly and in large quantities.
Prepare extra food for Uncle Harold; he eats like a horse.

eat one's cake and have it too
To be in the untenable position of consuming something while at the same time preserving it for future consumption.
It's difficult to enjoy shopping while also sticking to a strict budget; you can't eat your cake and have it too.

eat one's heart out
To experience self-inflicted internal suffering from conflicts involving jealousy, envy, and related emotions.
Bill secretly hoped his neighbor would eat his heart out when the new sports car arrived from the dealer.

eat one's words
To have the humbling experience of being forced to take back or repudiate what one has said.
The sports commentator had to eat her words when the youngest skater finished first.

eat out of one's hand
To cause another person to act as you wish.
The auctioneer soon had the bidders eating out of his hand.

(something) eats at one
Something irritates, nags at, or bothers one internally.
Memories of the argument continued to eat at Paul.

egg on one's face
The result of a mistake is linked directly to the person responsible for the mistake.

If we don't act quickly to solve this problem, we're all going to have egg on our faces.

eggs in one basket
All one's savings or hopes are in one investment (with danger implied).

The investment counselor warned us not to put all our eggs in one basket.

elbow grease
A substantial amount of manual work, such as scrubbing, polishing, or painting.

The apartment could be made quite presentable with a little elbow grease.

eleventh hour
The final opportunity for action.

You shouldn't have waited until the eleventh hour to express your concern.

emperor wears no clothes
What others claim exists does not in fact exist.

Although audiences applauded the famous actor's performance, the critics disagreed and claimed that the emperor wore no clothes.

every dog has its day
Brief periods of success come to even the least deserving.

We hated to see Sam win yet another hand of poker, but every dog has its day.

eye for an eye and a tooth for a tooth
Revenge is exacted in proportion to the injury received.

The soldiers vowed an eye for an eye and a tooth for a tooth if they were attacked.

eye of the beholder
That which is perceived depends on the perceiver, not on the object itself.

The value that one places on abstract art is very much in the eye of the beholder.

eye-to-eye
In accord and agreement.

Let's try to see eye-to-eye on the problem before we begin to discuss possible solutions.

eyeball-to-eyeball
In close personal confrontation, without intermediaries.

Furious, he demanded to meet his accusers eyeball-to-eyeball.

F

face the music

To confront rather than retreat from punishment, difficulty, or challenge.

They enjoyed charging the entire vacation on credit cards, but when they came home it was time to face the music and pay all those bills.

facts of life

Details of human sexuality; more generally, the way human existence proceeds.

It may seem unreasonable that large organizations often lose their competitive edge, but those are the facts of life.

fair-haired boy

The favorite.

Collin was the fair-haired boy in the office after closing four major sales in one week.

fake someone out

To deceive a person, usually by a sudden move or strategy.

Their stern looks were only an attempt to fake us out.

fall off the wagon

To return to a vice such as drunkenness.

We never expected the iron-willed Martin to fall off the wagon.

fall on one's face

To embarrass oneself by a highly visible failure.

No matter how much experience you've had in this business, it's still possible to fall on your face.

fall on one's sword

To commit suicide, real or symbolic.

Ignoring the client's clear wishes was Mark's way of falling on his sword as far as his professional life was concerned.

farm out

To subcontract or distribute to others.

Perhaps we can farm out some of our marketing studies.

fast and loose

Without regard for usual rules or morality.

I had the feeling the broker was playing fast and loose with our account.

fast buck

Money earned quickly and often illegally or immorally.

He grew up believing that the fast buck was the best route to financial security.

fast talker

A person adept at persuasive speaking but insincere and deceptive.

The musical featured a fast talker in a small town in the Midwest.

fast track

A route to rapid progress or promotion.

Three new MBAs have been placed on the fast track in the company.

fat is in the fire

A situation in which the most controversial, damning, or emotional aspects of a topic are revealed.

They tried to hide the candidate's excesses from the press, but now the fat is in the fire.

fate worse than death

An unimaginably horrific consequence or destiny.

Some avid skiers think of encountering an ice storm as a fate worse than death.

feather in one's cap

A sign of praiseworthy acts or accomplishments.

Receiving the mathematics medal during her senior year was a feather in Marlene's cap.

fed up with

Past the point of tolerance; exhaustion of patience.

Aren't you fed up with his constant efforts to take over your job duties?

feel blue

To experience sadness or melancholy.

We all feel blue from time to time and need cheering up.

feel no pain

To be inebriated or under the influence of drugs.

After his fifth glass of champagne, the groom was feeling no pain.

feel one's oats

To experience high levels of energy and excitement.

It was a pleasure to see the senior citizens feeling their oats on the outing.

feet of clay

Flawed aspects of character in a person generally thought to be admirable.

The leader hid his feet of clay from all but his closest associates.

few and far between

Scarce; rare.

Days of perfect weather are few and far between in Chicago.

fiddle while Rome burns

To occupy oneself with trivial amusements while a tragedy or disaster is taking place.

The CEO's lavish cocktail party for the board was a case of fiddling while Rome burns, given the problems the company faces.

fill the bill

To satisfy the requirements.

That set of golf clubs should fill the bill for the young professional.

filthy lucre
Money in general; sometimes used to refer to ill-gotten gain.
> *One speaker decried our culture for its obsession with filthy lucre.*

finger pointing
Accusing; blaming.
> *We've had enough finger pointing; now it's time for each of us to take personal responsibility for these problems.*

first come, first served
The first in order of arrival receives the first service.
> *The bakery advertised its Saturday sale on a first-come, first-served basis.*

fish or cut bait
To act or end one's participation.
> *Are you going to make an offer or not? It's time to fish or cut bait.*

fishing expedition
Any exploration or investigation lacking a specific target but hoping nonetheless to make relevant discoveries.
> *The FBI's investigation was more of a fishing expedition than a carefully planned search.*

fit as a fiddle
In good condition; often said of one's physical condition.
> *The octogenarian claimed to be fit as a fiddle and exercised every day.*

five-finger discount
Stealing by hand.
> *Three of the youngsters got candy by means of the five-finger discount.*

flake out

To take a nap; also, to shirk responsibility; prove unreliable.

After two exhaustive exams in the morning, the chemistry major flaked out all afternoon.

flash in the pan

Momentary, illusory sign of value or beauty.

Wendell's early successes proved to be merely a flash in the pan.

flat refusal

Unequivocal rejection or denial.

The labor leader issued a flat refusal to compromise her position.

flesh and blood

One's relatives, especially one's direct family.

How can you remain estranged from your own flesh and blood?

(to) flesh out

To give substance to; to elaborate.

All that remains for this presentation is to flesh out some of the smaller points.

fly by the seat of one's pants

To make decisions and base actions on intuition and impulse, not plan.

Especially during the first weeks on the job, you will feel that you are flying by the seat of your pants.

fly in the ointment

A disruptive element in an otherwise acceptable situation, substance, or circumstance.

The fly in the ointment of the new benefits package is the absence of a dental plan.

fly off the handle
To display sudden anger.
I really don't understand why he flies off the handle whenever the subject of raises comes up.

fly the coop
To suddenly leave a familiar place of residence or work.
Inevitably, children fly the coop to begin lives of their own.

food for thought
Subject worth considering.
Her talk gave us all food for thought.

fool's errand
A task only a foolish person would be given or would accept.
Trying to collect that bill from a bankrupt company is a fool's errand.

fools rush in
Rash people take impulsive actions that wiser people fear to take.
I don't agree with the CEO's sudden decision to open an office in Prague, but fools rush in.

foot in one's mouth
A glaring, embarrassing mistake in one's conversation or public speaking.
Her roommate couldn't forgive herself for sticking her foot in her mouth when she first met Ted.

foot in the door
A first stage or incursion in persuading or gaining access.
The free sample should give our company a foot in the door with the new client.

foot the bill
To pay the charges.
The company will foot the bill.

for all the tea in China
For any amount of material wealth.
He said he wouldn't change his mind for all the tea in China.

for peanuts
For relatively little money.
We can't ask college interns to work for peanuts.

for the birds
Not worth a person's time or energy.
No matter what others say, I think this ridiculous plan is for the birds.

forbidden fruit
Taboo but seductive lures.
Peter reached for the forbidden fruit of dating the boss's daughter.

fox is watching the henhouse
Responsibility for guardianship has been given over to the prime predator.
With his questionable reputation, appointing Quentin as a financial auditor is like asking the fox to watch the henhouse.

freak out
To experience sudden anxiety, panic, or disorientation, usually due to an unanticipated stimulus.
Don't freak out when you see our credit card bill this month.

free-for-all
An environment in which people act in the absence of rules or without regard for rules.
Bidding at the auction for the artifacts turned out to be a free-for-all with everyone shouting at once.

from hand to mouth
Obtaining sustenance on a day-by-day or hour-by-hour basis.

Before returning to school, he had been living from hand to mouth as a carpenter in Montana.

from scratch
From nothing or from inauspicious beginnings.

Her mother built this company from scratch.

from the ground up
From the earliest stages of growth.

We wanted to understand the development of the region from the ground up.

fudge factor
An allowable margin of error or forgiveness.

Fortunately, a fudge factor of about ten percent was secretly included in the deal.

(a) full plate
Much to do.

The administrator has a full plate next week.

(in) full swing
At the height of activity or involvement.

Seeing the debate program in full swing gave great joy to its founders.

G

gear up for
To prepare for; become equipped for.
Now it's time to gear up for winter weather.

get a fix on
To clarify, define, obtain clear focus on; achieve understanding of.
Before we settle on a price, let's get a fix on what competitors are asking.

get a grip
To regain control of one's emotions.
Henry, you have to get a grip before going back to discuss your feelings with the boss.

get a kick out of
To enjoy; find amusement or diversion in.
Grandparents always seem to get a kick out of even the simplest antics of their grandchildren.

get a move on
To hurry.
We have to get a move on if we're going to make our train.

get a rise out of
To get a reaction, especially a spontaneous reaction.
What do we have to do to get a rise out of that lazy gardener?

get away with murder
To avoid penalties or punishment for outrageous acts.
The town council let the mayor get away with murder in appointing friends and relatives to positions in city government.

get back on one's feet
To regain one's health, financial stability, or professional standing.
Federal loans helped the victims of the flood get back on their feet.

get down to brass tacks

To focus on basic issues.

After more than an hour of quibbling, the panelists finally got down to brass tacks.

get down to the nitty-gritty

To focus on core matters, including practical details.

I understand your general plan, but now let's get down to the nitty-gritty.

get in on the act

To participate; become involved.

After seeing the company-sponsored softball team's new uniforms, many employees wanted to get in on the act.

get in on the ground floor

To be an early or founding participant or investor in a growing venture.

Those who got in on the ground floor of the computer company ended up with a nice profit.

get in the groove

To put aside distractions and perform at one's best.

She usually plays tennis for an hour or so before she really gets in the groove.

get one's back (or dander) up

To become irritated or angry.

The news of yet another relocation for company headquarters got Ted's back up.

get one's feet wet

To become experienced, not merely knowledgable.

You can't get your feet wet from reading instruction manuals.

get one's goat

To arouse feelings of frustration or anger in a person.

The favoritism practiced in this organization really gets my goat.

get out of hand
To go beyond usual or expected boundaries or limits.
Don't let entertainment expenses for guests get out of hand.

get the ax
To be fired, terminated.
We heard that the last-hired employees would be the first to get the ax.

get to first base
To reach an initial stage of success.
In planning a cross-country bike trip, we have to get to first base by locating reliable equipment.

get wind of
To hear about; learn of.
Did you get wind of the governor's opposition to smoking in public buildings?

gild the lily
To attempt to enhance natural beauty through artificial means.
Saying more about Linda's many accomplishments would simply be gilding the lily.

give a hoot
To care about; be concerned over.
Few of us give a hoot about reading the employee handbook.

give it the once-over
To consider something in a cursory way.
She handed him the broken part and he gave it the once-over.

give no quarter
To give an adversary no advantage or respite.
In developing a hard-hitting advertising campaign, we must give no quarter to our competitors.

give one the boot
To fire; terminate; expel someone.
Unfortunately, we have to give one of the executives the boot before we can afford to hire more mid-level managers.

give one the brushoff
To dismiss someone's attentions, often without courtesy.
She gave David the brushoff after learning that he had no authority to make a deal.

give one the nod
To indicate preference for or choice of a person.
After an extensive search, the committee gave Paula the nod for the new position.

give the devil his due
To give credit where deserved even to disreputable sources.
Although we all disliked Calvin's management style, we had to give the devil his due in admitting that he achieved record production levels.

give the lie to
To show or prove the falsity of.
Your expression gives the lie to your words.

give the shirt off one's back
To be extraordinarily generous, to the point of self-sacrifice.
He is one of those rare people who will give you the shirt off his back.

give up the ghost
To die; have one's soul leave one's body.
I've got to have a drink of water before I give up the ghost.

give up the ship
To make the ultimate decision to let an enterprise or other situation fail.
Let's not give up the ship simply because we're experiencing a difficult period.

glaring falsehood
Gross untruth.

> *None of us expected a glaring falsehood from a public official.*

glue factory
Final, ignoble end (as in the case of horses sent at their death to the glue factory for processing).

> *If I can't work and can't play golf, I guess there's nothing left for me but the glue factory.*

glutton for punishment
One who seems to seek out pain, discomfort, penalties, or stress.

> *By asking for the most difficult work assignments, Priscilla became known throughout the company as a glutton for punishment.*

go down the drain
To be irretrievably lost.

> *All our hard work went down the drain when the stock market crashed.*

go dutch
To share the expense according to costs incurred by each.

> *Let's go dutch today, and I'll treat tomorrow.*

go fly a kite
To get away; amuse oneself elsewhere; leave.

> *She finally told the persistent door-to-door salesperson to go fly a kite.*

go for a spin
To take a short, usually pleasurable drive.

> *Are you interested in going for a spin in my new car?*

go haywire
When something or someone significantly malfunctions.

> *The central processing unit in the computer went haywire.*

go in one ear and out the other
To be heard but not remembered.
Her parents' advice went in one ear and out the other.

go into a tailspin
To start a downward course leading to destruction.
A mere rumor caused the company's stock to go into a tailspin.

go off half-cocked
To leave as if for action with only partial information or some wrong impressions.
The thorough training sessions prevented us from going off half-cocked without knowing our new product line well.

go off the deep end
To respond in an exaggerated, often destructive way.
Reacting with emotion is fine, but don't go off the deep end.

go overboard
To act excessively.
The neighbors went overboard in welcoming back the local Olympic medal winner.

go public
To share private information with the public.
A former administrative assistant threatened to go public with negative information.

go the extra mile
To perform beyond expectations, often in a selfless way.
Customers always remember the salesperson willing to go the extra mile.

go to one's head
To have one's egotism increase.
Don't let this string of successes go to your head.

go to school on
To learn from the observed experience of another.
One golfer went to school on another golfer's putt.

go to town
To become intensely active or involved.
Energized by the short vacation, company employees returned to work ready to go to town on the next project.

go underground
To become secretive, private, or guarded, especially in a conspiratorial way.
After being publicly ridiculed for their ideas, Malcolm and his friends went underground with their social politics.

go with the flow
To allow oneself to be influenced primarily by predominant movements, ideas, or social processes.
One way to avoid tension is to learn to go with the flow.

go without saying
Describing something so obvious it need not be said.
It goes without saying that guests should be treated well in one's home.

going like gangbusters
Performing with great enthusiasm and bravado.
The factory was going like gangbusters in the weeks just before Christmas.

golden opportunity
An especially advantageous chance for action.
Speaking occasions can be a golden opportunity to gain recognition for one's ideas.

golden parachute
Provisions for payments, benefits, and other desirable features as part of a retirement, termination, or resignation plan.
The CEO negotiated a golden parachute as part of her total compensation package.

goose egg
Zero; failure to accomplish anything.
> *After bold promises, the new supervisor laid a goose egg in failing to increase quarterly profits.*

grandstand play
An action calculated to attract attention and maximize focus on the central participant(s), often in a manipulative way.
> *Working as a team means that none of us will resort to grandstand plays as individuals.*

grasp at straws
To seek unlikely solutions in a desperate way.
> *By raising such trivial issues, you are merely grasping at straws.*

grass-roots level
The lowest level of authority in a hierarchy, often said of the common population.
> *Campaign funding should come from the grass-roots level, if possible.*

graveyard shift
Work hours spanning all or most of the night.
> *No one wanted to work the graveyard shift.*

gray area
A portion of a topic, issue, or other matter that remains ambiguous, undecided, or intractable for analysis.
> *All moral decisions seem to involve some gray area.*

grease one's palm
To pay one for favorable treatment.
> *To get a good table at the restaurant, you may have to grease the owner's palm.*

greased lightning
With extreme speed and suddenness.
> *She ran the sprint event like greased lightning.*

(get, give the) green light
To give the signal to proceed.
Don't begin work until I give you the green light.

grin and bear it
To hide one's feelings of disappointment or pain and
endure what must be endured.
*Even when a client is wrong, you may have to grin and
bear it.*

grind to a halt
To come to a stop in a gradual, laborious way.
All progress on the project began to grind to a halt.

growing pains
Discomfort or other undesirable sensations or reactions
associated with growth, especially of an organization or
person.
*I think the company is merely experiencing growing pains,
not severe problems.*

gum up the works
To act in such a way as to cripple or impede a process,
machine, or other system.
Your efforts to help are gumming up the works.

gun-shy
Fearful of participation in activity that has previously
been unsuccessful.
*He was gun-shy after his initial failure as an account
executive.*

H

habit of mind

The usual pattern of thinking.

Are you in the habit of mind of focusing on your successes or your failures?

hail-fellow-well-met

A spirit of hearty, enthusiastic greeting.

Rudy's spirit of hail-fellow-well-met worked well with new acquaintances, but became tiresome to old friends.

hair stand on end

Feelings of terror.

The movie about space aliens made my hair stand on end.

hale and hearty

Strong and healthy, often said of older people.

Her own father remained hale and hearty through his eighties.

half a mind

A decision or idea not yet completed that is formed in one's mind.

I have half a mind to sell this car and buy a bicycle.

hammer out

To produce with great effort and, often, implied conflict.

The negotiators worked all night to hammer out an acceptable agreement.

hand in the cookie jar

An effort to steal from a tempting resource.

The embezzler was caught with her hand in the cookie jar at the company.

hand over fist

With speed or intensity.

Gwen's fruit stand made money hand over fist during the summer months.

hand that rocks the cradle
Important early life influences, especially parental influence.
> *To explain her role as a stay-at-home mother, Hanna reminded us all of the hand that rocks the cradle.*

hands down
Without difficulty.
> *She won the competition hands down.*

hands-on
In an experiential way.
> *I prefer hands-on training to theoretical training.*

handwriting on the wall
Describing when the outcome of an event or other information is apparent.
> *We saw the handwriting on the wall when company profits began to fall.*

hang around
To remain at a location without a specific purpose or being involved in a particular activity; spending leisure time.
> *Do you want to walk to the park or just hang around the house?*

hang by a thread
To be almost entirely separated from the whole or one's source of security or sustenance.
> *His own job security hangs by a thread now that his boss has been fired.*

hang in the balance
To depend entirely upon.
> *The fate of the nation hangs in the balance.*

hang onto one's hat
To brace oneself for physical or mental action or surprise.
> *When Foley takes over a project, hang onto your hat!*

hang out one's shingle
To advertise one's services.
Do you plan to hang out your shingle immediately after graduation?

hanky-panky
Risqué or sexually oriented activity, especially in a work setting.
We all heard rumors of hanky-panky, but we had no direct evidence.

happy hunting ground
Good source; paradise.
Fred found that swap meets were the happy hunting ground for used computer parts.

hard-core
Uncensored and explicit, often said of pornography.
The Internet restricted access to hard-core sex sites.

hard-hitting
With substantial impact.
The journalist published a hard-hitting exposé on political corruption.

hard-nosed
Unrelenting; uncompromising.
Working for a hard-nosed boss taught us all the value of compassion.

hard row to hoe
Difficult tasks or fate faced by someone.
Lydia had a hard row to hoe from the time she was a girl in Memphis.

hard sell
Use of pressure tactics in persuasion.
Using the hard sell can alienate some customers.

(play) hardball
To use blunt, forceful techniques or language.
It's not necessary to play hardball to get your point across.

(wouldn't) harm a fly
Gentle; harmless.
In spite of his huge size, Jason wouldn't harm a fly.

harp on a point
To return to an issue again and again.
One city council member insists on harping on a point until he gets his way.

has-been
Person whose time of importance has passed.
Morley is a has-been in business circles, but still exerts considerable influence socially.

haste makes waste
Hurrying causes poor use of resources.
Even at times of a company crisis, we tried to concentrate on our work and remember that haste makes waste.

haul (or rake) over the coals
To put one under painful or torturous scrutiny or punishment.
Thornton was called into the boss's office to be hauled over the coals regarding the company dress code.

have a ball
To enjoy thoroughly.
We want you to relax and have a ball.

have a blast
To enjoy with great enthusiasm and energy.
The children plan to have a blast at the amusement park.

have a field day

To enjoy with sensations of triumph.

Our competitors are going to have a field day with this news of our product failure.

have a good head on one's shoulders

To be wise, smart, possessed of good common sense.

Natalie is respected not only for her technical skills but also for having a good head on her shoulders.

have a leg up

To possess an advantage due to help received.

Employees with degrees in computer science have a leg up on the rest of us in learning new computer languages.

have a mind of one's own

To be an independent thinker, forming one's own opinions.

From her earliest years, Maddie definitely had a mind of her own.

have it made in the shade

To attain success without much stress.

Thanks to the large inheritance, the young couple felt they had it made in the shade.

have money to burn

To possess so much money that one can waste some of it without concern.

All the members of the exclusive club gave the impression that they had money to burn.

have someone dead to rights

To demonstrate or prove a person's guilt, responsibility, or involvement with absolute certainty, allowing no excuse or appeal.

The thief thought he had a solid alibi, but the district attorney eventually had him dead to rights.

head over heels
Completely; with abandon.
> *They were clearly* head over heels *in love with one another.*

head-to-head
Direct confrontation.
> *The Superbowl promised* head-to-head *combat between the country's best football teams.*

heads-up
Alert; smart.
> *By locating the problem and stopping the assembly line, Jacob made a* heads-up *play.*

hear a pin drop
To be in a very quiet environment.
> *It was so quiet that you could* hear a pin drop.

(one's) heart goes out to
To empathize with.
> *My* heart goes out to *all those who lost relatives in the disaster.*

heart of gold
Having consistently good intentions, with the implication of selflessness.
> *He has a gruff exterior but a* heart of gold.

heart-to-heart (talk)
Emotionally honest, with candid disclosure of true feelings.
> *We eventually had a chance to have a* heart-to-heart talk *with our family physician.*

hellfire and brimstone
Threats of impending punishment or pain.
> Hellfire and brimstone *preaching still holds large audiences spellbound and trembling.*

henpecked
Constantly criticized or reminded of obligations,
especially domestic ones.
*Henpecked husbands are no more common than henpecked
wives.*

here today, gone tomorrow
The transitory nature of life.
*Without any sign of serious illness, Victor was here today,
gone tomorrow.*

high and dry
Out of one's element; without recourse.
*The bankruptcy of the tour company left the tourists high
and dry in a foreign country.*

high as a kite
At an extreme level; often said of excitement or
drunkenness.
*Ben felt high as a kite after his first deep-sea diving
experience.*

high roller
One who gambles for large stakes.
*His aunt dresses and acts like a high roller when she visits
Atlantic City.*

high sign
The signal to take or cease action.
*The foreman will give you the high sign before the truck
begins to unload.*

highway robbery
Outrageous fees that seem tantamount to stealing.
*Their prices are highway robbery compared to what we pay
for the same merchandise elsewhere.*

hill of beans
Something small and insignificant.
His objections didn't amount to a hill of beans.

hint of trouble

A sign or symptom of difficulty or problems.

At the first hint of trouble, take the car to a qualified mechanic.

hit-or-miss

Extremely inconsistent.

Her tactics in marketing were hit-or-miss.

hit pay dirt

To reach the source of success or riches.

After filing more than twenty patents, Sally finally hit pay dirt.

hit the books

To study, with intensity implied.

Few of us will pass the examination unless we hit the books over the weekend.

hit the ceiling

To show sudden anger.

When she saw the broken window, she hit the ceiling.

hit the deck

To throw oneself down quickly on one's stomach.

If bullets begin to fly, hit the deck.

hit the fan

To have problems impact in a sudden way.

Problems were building in the office and finally hit the fan on a hot Friday afternoon.

hit the hay

To go to bed.

After a bumpy flight, Hank opted to hit the hay early.

hit the nail on the head

To state an issue or other matter with precision.

Although he lacked a technical vocabulary, the mechanic hit the nail on the head in describing the automotive problem.

hit the road
To leave, with an emotional component or attitude implied.
Lauren told the unwelcome visitor to hit the road.

hit the skids
To experience a period of severe deterioration or misfortune.
By the end of the year, the struggling company had hit the skids.

hit the spot
To prove satisfying.
The cool water from the spring hit the spot on the warm afternoon.

hold a candle to
To compare to.
His management skills can't hold a candle to hers.

hold down the fort
To maintain the usual functioning and stability of a place during another's absence.
While we go shopping, you can hold down the fort here at home.

hold one's fire
To cease aggression or action.
Hold your fire until we determine who's at fault.

hold one's horses
To stop forward motion, including mental functions such as planning.
Hold your horses if you see any sign that the children are becoming frightened.

hold one's tongue
To remain silent when one is tempted to speak.
Brent had learned every business skill except how to hold his tongue.

hold onto your hat

To prepare oneself for surprising experience of some kind.

If you haven't seen today's headline, hold onto your hat.

hold out an olive branch

To offer compromise or extend overtures of peacemaking.

The ambassador agreed to hold out an olive branch to the foreign country if it would renounce the development of atomic weapons.

hold the bag

To be given responsibility for, or consequences of, often unwittingly.

Even though he wasn't involved in planning the robbery, Oliver was left holding the bag.

hold the line

To allow no changes in something.

The new budget cuts mean that we will all have to hold the line on spending.

hook, line, and sinker

Entirely; without hesitation.

He accepted our ideas hook, line, and sinker.

(by) hook or (by) crook

One way or another, regardless of morality.

We have to find financing for the project by hook or by crook.

horns of a dilemma

Problematic choices or alternatives.

The new information about pollution control made the legislators feel they were on the horns of a dilemma.

horse around

To play, with the implication of spontaneity (without the rules of a game).

The older children began to horse around in the backyard while the younger children played in the nursery.

horse of a different color
An entirely different matter.
Changing careers after fifty is a horse of a different color.

(from the) horse's mouth
From the original source.
We heard about the deal straight from the horse's mouth—the president of the company.

hot off the press
Recently published, just made known.
This news is hot off the press.

hot potato
An item that will cause damage or pain if held too long, hence the temptation to give it to someone else.
The question of Mel's eligibility for promotion was a political hot potato in the company.

hot under the collar
Angry.
Her lack of gratitude made Martha hot under the collar.

(tumbling down like a) house of cards
Sudden collapse involving all aspects of the structure or situation.
When the embezzlement became known, the company's reputation came tumbling down like a house of cards.

hue and cry
Loud objections; uproar.
The governor shouted for quiet above the hue and cry of questions from reporters.

I

if the shoe fits, wear it
If an accusation against one is accurate, one should
own up to it.
> *You may not be responsible for damage to the neighbor's
> fence, but if the shoe fits, wear it.*

in a jam
In trouble.
> *I'm in a jam and need help immediately.*

in a New York minute
Right away; in a hurry.
> *I would take advantage of that opportunity in a New
> York minute.*

in a nutshell
In a concise or abbreviated form.
> *Here's the idea in a nutshell.*

in bed together
In collusion with; sharing with.
> *The mayor and the city council are in bed together on
> this issue.*

in cahoots with
In collusion with; sharing with.
> *The sheriff was in cahoots with two felons.*

in cold blood
Brutally; without sympathy or remorse.
> *He shot the man in cold blood.*

in like Flynn
Completely accepted or empowered.
> *After our introduction by the president of the company, we
> felt we were in like Flynn.*

in seventh heaven
In a state of ecstasy.
> *She was in seventh heaven every time she looked at her engagement ring.*

in the bag
Successfully concluded; no longer at risk.
> *Unless unforeseen problems develop, this deal is in the bag.*

in the clouds
Impractical; dreamy.
> *The professor knew her subject, but she seemed in the clouds to many students.*

in the doghouse
In trouble, usually due to domestic disputes.
> *Ralph found himself in the doghouse after forgetting an anniversary.*

in the driver's seat
In control.
> *Where a company goes depends in large part on who's in the driver's seat.*

in the know
Having full or additional knowledge.
> *Only those in the know have taken advantage of this opportunity.*

in the limelight
Having public attention focused on one.
> *Placing oneself in the limelight often invites unexpected problems.*

in the long run
When considered over an extended period of time.
> *Her policies will probably prove wise in the long run.*

in the neighborhood of
Approximately.
We'd like to spend an amount in the neighborhood of $150,000.

in the nick of time
At the last possible moment.
The car crossed the railroad tracks just in the nick of time before the train roared by.

in the red
At a financial loss.
Company financial records showed two divisions to be in the red.

in the thick of
At the most intense period or part of something.
We stopped by our friends' home and found them in the thick of an argument.

in the trenches
In the most difficult, trying environment.
The struggle to gain market share will be won in the trenches of one-to-one selling.

including the kitchen sink
Everything, down to the last item.
Jenson packed everything including the kitchen sink into his recreational vehicle before leaving for Arizona.

iron out difficulties
To solve problems; smooth over differences.
I want to iron out any difficulties that may have occurred during my absence.

(too many) irons in the fire
Being over-extended in one's interests or commitments.
Some problems took place because Wilma had too many irons in the fire.

it never rains but it pours
Something that comes too often arrives in overabundance.
As is usual with bad luck, it never rains but it pours.

it takes two to tango
Two parties, not one, are involved and responsible.
Before you blame Richard entirely, remember that it takes two to tango.

it's Greek to me
I don't understand.
I studied the computer manual for an hour, but it was Greek to me.

ivory tower
An area removed from the real world and negatively characterized for its impractical influence.
He left his ivory tower in academia to take a difficult but profitable job in industry.

J

jack-of-all-trades, master of none
One who does many things, but none of them well.
The house bore shabby testimony to its construction by a jack-of-all-trades, master of none.

jig is up
Deception or trickery is revealed.
Now that he has confessed, the jig is up.

(one's) John Hancock
One's signature.
Please put your John Hancock on the dotted line.

John Q. Public
The average citizen.
Politicians may view the problem one way, but John Q. Public sees it in an entirely different light.

Johnnie-come-lately
One who arrives (often purposely) after important events or developments have taken place and tries nevertheless to reap the benefits of those events or developments.
Any well-publicized company success brings a Johnnie-come-lately who is eager to claim partial credit.

joined at the hip
Very closely associated; loyal to one another.
He and his fraternity brothers are joined at the hip.

joyride
An automobile drive characterized by fun to the point of wildness or recklessness.
The parents worried that their teenagers' joyride might end in tragedy.

jump-start (someone or something)
To apply a burst of energy to motivate immediate action.
Company managers sought ways to jump-start the long-delayed supersonic jet project.

jump through a hoop
To perform an unnecessary obligation or task.
The scoutmaster was disliked because he made new troop members jump through hoops before allowing them to go on hikes.

junk food
Snack or fast food of low nutritional value.
Most of the students preferred junk food to cafeteria fare.

just fell off the turnip truck
Naive; unacquainted with urban ways.
Even though I'm from the country, don't think I just fell off the turnip truck.

K

keep a lid on
To not reveal; keep private.
I'll tell you a secret if you promise to keep a lid on it.

keep a stiff upper lip
To maintain one's courage.
The British are rightly famous for keeping a stiff upper lip through adverse times.

keep all balls in the air
To not let any of one's obligations be slighted or forgotten.
The office manager prided herself on keeping all balls in the air at the same time.

keep in touch with
To remain in contact with.
Although we will be living in distant cities, I hope we will keep in touch with one another.

keep the peace
To maintain friendly relationships.
At some family gatherings it becomes difficult to keep the peace.

keep the wolf from the door
To provide sufficient income and other forms of support to sustain the home or other entity.
Especially in urban areas, economic conditions often require both husband and wife to work to keep the wolf from the door.

keys to the kingdom
Access to available resources, with honor implied.
Based on the enthusiastic welcome by the president, you would think that the new executive vice president had been given the keys to the kingdom.

kick the bucket
To die, with lack of respect implied.
The mean old man finally kicked the bucket after a long and eventful life.

kick the habit
To free oneself from a strong predeliction or addiction.
Substance abusers rarely have success in kicking the habit on the first try.

kick the tires
To perform rudimentary tests on a product prior to purchasing it.
Before making any purchase, be sure to look it over carefully and kick the tires.

kick up one's heels
To celebrate in a physically active way.
The monthly dances at the retirement home gave residents a chance to kick up their heels.

kill time
To perform relatively purposeless activities in order to help time pass.
One popular way to kill time is to watch daytime TV shows.

kill two birds with one stone
To accomplish two purposes with one effort or action.
By buying a cat to rid the house of mice and to serve as a pet, we killed two birds with one stone.

king's ransom
A vast amount of money.
Homes in that neighborhood must cost a king's ransom.

knock on wood
Trying to ward off misfortune and invite good luck.
I hope we all have a healthy new year, knock on wood.

knock-down-drag-out fight
A conflict characterized by brutal struggle.
Expect a knock-down-drag-out fight the next time our management committee tries to decide on a merit pay plan.

knuckle down
To bear down intensely.
By knuckling down to our work, we can complete it well before the deadline.

knuckle under
To give in; surrender to.
Mike would not knuckle under to Conrad's unreasonable demands.

know which side one's bread is buttered on
To know from what source one's benefits come.
She seems politically astute and knows which side her bread is buttered on.

L

labor of love
A work done for the satisfaction one finds in it.
The sculpture was a labor of love, not a work for profit.

lame duck
One still in service but whose removal from service has already been determined.
The congressional representative remained on in Washington as a lame duck for almost a year.

land of milk and honey
Paradise or paradise-like state.
In captivity, the Jewish people looked forward to their eventual journey to the land of milk and honey.

land-office business
A high-volume, high-profit, and frenetic trading environment.
The garment outlet store did a land-office business during tourist season.

land on one's feet
To recover from an upset without lasting damage.
One's character can often be measured by the grace with which one lands on one's feet after an unexpected upset.

land the job
To be hired.
William celebrated after landing the job he wanted.

larger than life
Exaggerated in characteristics and attributes.
Sandra's voice, gestures, and expressions were all larger than life.

last roundup
The moment of death; final time of accounting.
After the ten-mile hike across the mountain, we felt we were headed toward the last roundup.

last straw

The final event, irritation, or other stimulus that leads to a reaction.

Matthew's sarcastic comment at the board meeting was the last straw for the president of the company.

laugh all the way to the bank

To show no remorse (but instead, glee) over the way in which one has obtained money, even in ways that others disapprove of.

Fran has been criticized for her type of work, but she laughs all the way to the bank.

laugh up one's sleeve

To hide the expression of one's amusement.

Georgia could not help but laugh up her sleeve as the consultant went on and on with promises of what he could do for the company.

laundry list

A long list of items.

The coach had a laundry list of comments and criticisms after watching a videotape of the game.

lay an egg

To fail; perform poorly.

After two previous failures, we can't afford to lay an egg this time.

lay down the law

To forcefully set forth unambiguous rules or commands.

Tough love sometimes means laying down the law to loved ones.

lay off

To terminate one's job temporarily until such time as the person can be hired.

Two corporations pledged not to lay off employees without at least six months' severance pay.

lead by the nose

To be extremely overt and obvious in guiding a person to a particular conclusion or course of action.

You do not have to lead me by the nose to persuade me to buy your product.

lease on life

A time to live.

The vitamins seemed to give Mindy a new lease on life.

leave in the lurch

To abandon at a time of great need or urgency.

By quitting when he did, Trenton managed to leave us all in the lurch.

leave no stone unturned

To investigate all clues; explore all options.

The police lieutenant ordered her troops to leave no stone unturned in looking for the lost child.

left-handed compliment

Apparent praise that actually contains an insult or criticism.

His comment that her one-of-a-kind hairstyle was "unusual" was a left-handed compliment.

(a) leg up on

An advantage due to help received.

His solid background in electrical engineering gives Cal a leg up on others in the systems design department.

let off steam

To vent one's anger or frustration.

It's healthy to let off steam rather than letting anger smolder within.

let one's hair down

To relax; become informal and comfortable.

After work, Mary's boyfriend urged her to let her hair down and relax.

let the cat out of the bag
To reveal a secret.
You spoiled her surprise party by letting the cat out of the bag.

let the chips fall where they may
To allow the results of an action to occur, no matter what or whom is impacted.
His advice was to act honestly and openly, then to let the chips fall where they may.

level best
One's best effort.
You will seldom go wrong by trying your level best.

life of the party
One whose antics and humor make a party particularly lively.
Nick was the life of the party until he fell into the swimming pool.

light of day
Dawn; enlightenment generally.
We have talked and talked, but we can't make him see the light of day.

lightning never strikes twice in the same spot
An unusual occurrence that once experienced by a person, will not happen again for that person.
The chances that Bob will have a repeat encounter with a bear are remote; lightning never strikes twice in the same spot.

like a house on fire
With great energy.
They were working like a house on fire in an effort to finish the report before the sales meeting.

(a) likely story
A story fabricated to serve one's interests; said when a story is not believed.
Your alibi is a likely story; I find it hard to accept.

lip service
Words spoken but not meant.
> *They all paid lip service to the value of teleconferencing, but few used it.*

litany of excuses
An extended list of reasons and explanations.
> *We heard a litany of excuses on why Harold could not travel on weekends.*

little black book
A private directory of personal (often intimate) friends.
> *Jim's little black book got him into trouble when it fell into the wrong hands.*

live high on the hog
To live an extravagant lifestyle.
> *When crops were good, the farming community lived high on the hog.*

lock, stock, and barrel
All possessions and accoutrements.
> *He sold the delicatessen lock, stock, and barrel.*

long shot
A choice, option, or alternative that is unlikely to succeed.
> *His chances of becoming a corporate director are a long shot at best.*

look a gift horse in the mouth
To be unreceptive and ungrateful to one's benefactor.
> *In considering whether to accept the Employee of the Month bonus, don't look a gift horse in the mouth.*

look for a needle in a haystack
Search futilely for a small item hidden in a larger environment.
> *Trying to locate a bug in the computer program is like looking for a needle in a haystack.*

look one in the eye
To confront one directly and frankly.
Can he look you in the eye and tell you he didn't do it?

look through rose-colored glasses
To view life in a way distorted by one's mindset or emotions.
Mabel viewed the world through rose-colored glasses and never seemed to recognize the seriousness of the problems all around her.

loose cannon
People or things that are dangerous because of their unpredictability.
Barbara is highly skilled, but her volatile nature makes her a loose cannon in the company.

loose lips sink ships
Revealing secrets can cause disasters.
Revealing proprietary information can be damaging; remember—loose lips sink ships.

loosen (tighten) the purse strings
To spend more (less) money.
The boss will have to loosen the purse strings if she expects real progress on this project.

lord it over
To act superior in the presence of, or because of, a particular triumph.
Jack has no reason to lord it over the rest of us, even though he did receive a larger bonus.

lose heart
To give up courage and commitment.
Don't lose heart when temporary conditions are not to your liking.

lose one's marbles
To become unbalanced.
> *Unrelieved stress can eventually cause one to lose one's marbles.*

lose one's shirt
To sustain major financial losses.
> *Jackson lost his shirt in a particularly risky investment.*

luck of the draw
Fortune or misfortune based solely on chance.
> *By luck of the draw, he was selected for the trip to England.*

lump in one's throat
A sensation of strong emotion, as if one is about to cry.
> *The story of Marty's problems brought a lump to my throat.*

M

mad as a hatter
Crazy, in a bizarre (but usually not dangerous) way.
We all liked Paul, but at the same time felt that he was mad as a hatter.

mad as a hornet
Furious.
The marketing director burst out of the meeting room, mad as a hornet.

magic bullet
A miraculous solution to a problem.
Many employees consider the buy-out plan a magic bullet for saving their pensions.

make a clean breast
To disclose honestly and completely.
The simplest approach to conflict resolution is to make a clean breast of your own motives and actions.

make a killing
To achieve extremely large financial gains or other successes.
Everyone wants to make a killing in the stock market, but few have the patience and skill to do so.

make a long story short
To get right to the main point of a story.
To make a long story short, the hero returns to his tribe at the end of the movie.

make a monkey of
To make someone look foolish.
If her comments were intended to make a monkey out of Underwood, they succeeded.

make a mountain out of a molehill
To give unwarranted significance to something trivial.
We would need fewer meetings if some employees decided not to make mountains out of molehills.

make a splash

To make a sudden, usually positive impression.

The new sports center attempted to make a splash by offering free memberships for forty-eight hours.

make both ends meet

To spend no more money than one earns.

All members of the family contributed to help make both ends meet.

make hay while the sun shines

To do purposeful activity or enjoy oneself while conditions permit.

We knew we had to make hay while the sun shines, especially because a strike action threatened to shut down the factory within a matter of weeks.

make no bones about it

To not dissemble or elaborate unnecessarily.

I will make no bones about it: the city manager has been accepting bribes.

make one tick

To explain one's nature and actions.

Nathan was widely admired, but none of us knew exactly what made him tick.

make one's mark

To achieve at a level that wins public notice.

Of the many ways to make one's mark, law and medicine have traditionally been popular.

make waves

To disturb an otherwise calm situation.

Sometimes it is necessary to make waves in order to call attention to an important problem.

meet one's match
To come up against a person who is as good as one, and often better than one, at a given activity or in particular qualities.

It's not easy to remain confident once a person meets his or her match.

meet one's Waterloo
To encounter an event that proves to be one's downfall.

Because of the hostile takeover, the CEO met his Waterloo.

meeting of the minds
An agreement among parties.

Before proceeding to the details of this settlement, let's make sure we have a meeting of the minds on the salary issue.

mellow out
To become relaxed and calm.

After a stressful day, the workers mellowed out by playing cards and drinking beer.

mending fences
Repairing damaged relationships.

Mending fences quickly is never so important as when friendships have been damaged over misunderstandings.

mental giant
A person of extraordinary intelligence.

Henderson was physically unimpressive but he had the well-deserved reputation of being a mental giant.

milk of human kindness
Good deeds accompanied by the best of motives.

As terrible as the disaster was for many families, it nevertheless brought forth the milk of human kindness in many ways.

millstone around one's neck
A seemingly inescapable event, obligation, or other experience that causes one problems; a heavy burden.
Gwendolyn felt that her parental obligations were a millstone around her neck when it came to pursuing a career in the theater.

mind like a steel trap
Being quick-thinking.
The precocious child had a mind like a steel trap.

mind one's p's and q's
To pay attention to all details, including aspects of one's behavior.
You have been given permission to enter the research facility, but mind your p's and q's in the laboratory areas.

miss one's bet
To guess incorrectly.
Unless I miss my bet, Vicky will be chosen as our PTA president next year.

money doesn't grow on trees
Money is not easy to get.
Her mother gave her $20, along with the admonition to spend it wisely because money doesn't grow on trees.

money in the bank
A reward or other gain that is assured and cannot be withheld.
His performance contract with Universal Bookings was money in the bank.

monkey on one's back
An unwanted obligation, task, responsibility, or problem.
You shifted responsibility to me for the project, and now the monkey is on my back.

month of Sundays
An impossibly long period of time.
> *He couldn't lose that much weight in a month of Sundays.*

more heat than light
More emotional venting than enlightenment.
> *They debated for hours, with more heat than light.*

more the merrier
The more people in attendance, the happier the occasion.
> *Of course you can invite your friends—the more the merrier.*

mouthpiece for
A spokesperson for.
> *The lawyer was notorious as a mouthpiece for organized crime.*

mover and shaker
One who is a major influence, especially in political, social, or business life.
> *For three generations, the family has been a mover and shaker in the Seattle area.*

muddy the waters
To obscure the issue.
> *Your many examples are intended to clarify your point, but they end up muddying the waters.*

N

nail someone to a cross

To punish someone cruelly in a publicly visible way.

When problems occur in business, it does little good to nail any one person to a cross.

name in lights

Attainment of fame, especially in the entertainment field.

With luck, she will soon see her name in lights.

necessary evil

A bad component required for the success of a plan.

Weekend travel is a necessary evil for many executives.

neck of the woods

Locale; area; neighborhood.

In this neck of the woods, we always hunt for food, never simply for pleasure.

nip in the bud

To stop something just as it begins.

Your dog's tendency to bite is a bad habit that you will definitely want to nip in the bud.

no pain, no gain

One cannot make progress without experiencing discomfort.

The dieters complained bitterly about the sparse menu, only to be counseled: "No pain, no gain."

nodding acquaintance

Someone known casually but not as a friend.

She had only a nodding acquaintance with the judge.

(have one's) nose out of joint

To become irritated or angry.

There's no reason to have your nose out of joint over your neighbor's innocent remark.

not over until the fat lady sings
Results cannot be called final until the very last moment.

> *We're behind by three runs, but it's not over until the fat lady sings.*

not to be sneezed at
Not to be treated lightly.

> *The pay offered for the position is not to be sneezed at.*

not too shabby
Impressive; used ironically to indicate just the opposite of shabby or run-down.

> *The interior of the luxuriously appointed yacht was not too shabby.*

not worth a plugged nickel
Worthless.

> *Those old stock certificates are not worth a plugged nickel.*

note of concern
An expression of caring or worry.

> *Do I detect a note of concern in your comments about Mother's health?*

nuggets of information
Bits of especially valuable or titillating information.

> *The brief interview yielded valuable nuggets of information.*

nurse a grudge
To concentrate on and retain the ill feelings one person has toward another who has wronged him or her.

> *Nursing a grudge consumes enormous emotional energy and pays few dividends.*

O

odd duck

A person with strange personality features.

Some of the world's most famous people are odd ducks in their private lives.

off base

Outside the rules or standards.

His comments were far off base with regard to David's character.

off one's chest

Relief experienced from disclosure or confession.

It must be a relief to get those feelings off your chest.

off one's rocker

Crazy; mentally imbalanced.

I believe he went off his rocker after the tragic accident.

off the bat

Suddenly; right away.

He couldn't give a firm opinion right off the bat.

off the beaten track

In a locale or region that is not well known.

The village is a bit off the beaten track, but well worth the visit.

off the cuff

Candidly; without preparation.

The remarks, which the speaker said were off the cuff, lasted more than an hour.

off the top of one's head

First thoughts or words, without thorough consideration or preparation.

Just off the top of her head, the physician could not think of a reason why the skin rash should recur so soon.

off the wagon
Back to a former state of drunkenness or other debilitating state.
We all felt discouraged when we heard that Richard had fallen off the wagon again.

off the wall
Unexpected; original; unique.
This idea may strike you as off the wall, but hear me out nonetheless.

old college try
Effort and enthusiasm reminiscent of college sports.
By giving this project the old college try, we may be able to finish by the deadline.

old hat
Stale; already done.
His ideas, no matter how well-expressed, are still old hat.

on a shoestring
On meager resources.
This company can't survive more than six months if we continue to run it on a shoestring.

on one's coattails
On someone else's accomplishments or reputation.
Bob felt that several coworkers were attempting to ride on his coattails after his Nobel Prize was awarded.

on the blink
Not operating correctly.
The refrigerator has been on the blink since June.

on the chopping block
Set for destruction or division.
One of our companies will be placed on the chopping block soon and massive layoffs will probably result.

on the dot
Precisely.
> *She left work at 5:00 P.M. on the dot.*

on the double
Quickly.
> *After hearing the fire alarm, we all exited the building on the double.*

on the fly
Performed rapidly while engaged with another activity.
> *I can put together some figures for you, but they will have to be done on the fly.*

on the fritz
Not operating correctly.
> *This TV has been on the fritz for weeks.*

on the lam
Running from the authorities.
> *The felon is on the lam, but police feel they have clues as to his whereabouts.*

on the mend
Healing or recovering.
> *Richard's wife is already out of the hospital and he, too, is on the mend.*

on the Q.T.
In secret; a private communication.
> *Strictly on the Q.T., I heard that one of our vice presidents is facing a major lawsuit.*

on the sidelines
Not a primary participant; someone awaiting the call to action.
> *He and his staff are on the sidelines for now, but just until our federal grant is renewed.*

on the sly
Secretly; in a stealthful way.
At their wedding, they admitted they had been dating on the sly much longer than any of us knew.

on the wagon
Recovering from a former state of drunkenness or other debilitation.
Sylvia is an excellent manager so long as she stays on the wagon.

on the warpath
In a mode of aggression, hostility, or anger.
The commander was on the warpath for soldiers who were off base without permission.

once in a blue moon
Rarely.
These opportunities arrive only once in a blue moon.

one fell swoop
Immediately; in one dramatic or intense action.
He managed to hire away all the competition's best employees in one fell swoop.

one for the books
Worth remembering; classic.
The announcer called the well-played game "one for the books."

one for the road
A drink to prepare one for a journey.
I have to go soon, but let's have one for the road.

one in a million
Someone or something very special.
The whole family agreed that Aunt Rose was one in a million.

one-night stand
A brief tryst, without a long-term relationship; by extension, any brief encounter.

> *When we sell to customers, we don't want them to feel they have experienced a one-night stand.*

open door policy
Open access provided by an authority figure as a means of obtaining feedback and other information from subordinates.

> *All senior administrators are required to maintain an open door policy from 1:00 P.M. to 5:00 P.M. on Friday afternoons.*

open secret
Something reputed to be secret, but is in fact, well known.

> *It's an open secret that no one ever gets fired at the post office.*

opportunity knocks
The chance for advantageous business action presents itself.

> *In this case, I truly believe that opportunity knocks, especially because so little risk is involved.*

out of gas
Depleted; exhausted.

> *Our venture started well but soon ran out of gas as its principals lost interest.*

out of one's shell
Overcoming one's shyness.

> *Games have a way of bringing people out of their shells at parties.*

out of the blue
Unexpectedly; from an unknown or unanticipated source.

> *The invitation to attend the inauguration came entirely out of the blue.*

out of the frying pan into the fire
From a bad situation to a worse one.
His lateral move from Accounting to Finance took him out of the frying pan into the fire.

out of the loop
Not sharing important information.
Andrew said he wanted to participate more fully, but felt out of the loop.

out of thin air
Appearing miraculously, unexpectedly, apparently without a known or anticipated source or origin.
Geniuses seem to have the ability to pull solutions to complex problems out of thin air.

out of this world
Amazing; extraordinary; remarkable.
The food at La Bomba Restaurant is out of this world.

out of touch
Not current or up to date; not meaningfully connected.
The longer she served in her leadership role, the more out of touch she became with those she led.

out on a limb
In a precarious and dangerous position.
Buying a second home puts us out on a limb financially.

out to lunch
Strange in personality or behavior; imbalanced.
I'm fond of her aunt, but his uncle is definitely out to lunch.

out to pasture
No longer active; retired.
Since the company can no longer afford him, perhaps it's time to put him out to pasture.

over a barrel

In a position necessitating concession or surrender.

The bargaining unit had management over a barrel when it came to the issue of on-site childcare arrangements.

over the long haul

In the long term.

Mentoring in corporations pays its richest dividends over the long haul.

P

packed like sardines
Positioned uncomfortably close to one another.
Even though the aircraft was new, the passengers felt packed like sardines in economy class.

paint oneself into a corner
To leave oneself no options.
If you do not watch your words and actions carefully, you may end up painting yourself into a corner.

paint the town red
To celebrate, especially by frequenting several bars and clubs in succession.
After hearing of her promotion, Inez and her friends went out to paint the town red.

pandemonium reigned
There is widespread chaos and extreme social disorder.
In the movie, news of an approaching asteroid terrified the population and pandemonium reigned.

paper it over
To cover up but not repair.
The minivan has some design flaws, but we can paper them over cosmetically.

paper tiger
A harmless version of something to be feared.
The lawyer, together with all his threats, proved to be no more than a paper tiger.

par for the course
Something that is to be expected.
He earned $65,000 in commissions—about par for the course for junior salespeople.

pass muster
To meet standards required for acceptance.
I wonder if the majority of high school graduates can pass muster in basic arithmetic.

pass the ball
To give responsibility or opportunity to someone else.
You're a natural leader but you still have to learn to pass the ball more.

pass the buck
To shirk blame or responsibility by assigning it to another person.
When she asked Henderson to authorize the expenditure, he passed the buck to his boss.

pay one's dues
To put in a period of required or expected work; experience an accepted degree of difficulty.
As one who has been with the company during its toughest times, you have certainly paid your dues.

pay the piper
To give money or other tribute to one who has provided delight or entertainment; to pay for one's pleasure.
We have all enjoyed ourselves, but now it's time to pay the piper.

pedal to the metal
To drive as fast as possible.
The young woman put her Mercedes pedal to the metal whenever she had the opportunity.

penny for one's thoughts
A request to share what one is thinking.
You seem contemplative—here's a penny for your thoughts.

penny-wise and pound-foolish
Overly concerned with small expenditures but oblivious to large expenditures.
Buying plastic furniture for the cafeteria is being penny-wise and pound-foolish; it will hold up only a year or two.

pet peeve
A relatively trivial frustration or complaint that one brings up often.
> *One of Jack's pet peeves was the absence of babies' changing tables in men's restrooms at the airport.*

peter out
End by gradually becoming less and less.
> *The vein of gold looked promising, but petered out a few yards from where it was discovered.*

photo finish
Result when two competitors reach a goal at what appears to be the same time.
> *The two runners crossed the line in a photo finish after ten kilometers.*

pick of the litter
The best among several alternatives.
> *There are many to choose from, but I think you've selected the pick of the litter.*

pick the brains
To solicit information or expertise.
> *The company sent invitations to several renowned scientists in hopes of picking their brains at the annual company meeting.*

pick up the tab
To pay the bill.
> *The company will pick up the tab for the outing.*

(a) picture is worth a thousand words
It would take a great deal of language to create the same impact as one picture.
> *Include more graphics in your report; a picture is worth a thousand words.*

pie in the sky
A reward so remote that it can never be obtained.
Accepting stock options in place of salary turns out to be pie-in-the-sky thinking for most workers.

piece of cake
Something easy.
The good student felt the exam was a piece of cake.

pipe dream
A fantasy unlikely to be made real.
I don't think we want to base an entire design on one engineer's pipe dream.

play cat and mouse
To tease.
Nick didn't resist negotiating, but neither did he want the company to play cat and mouse with him.

play fast and loose
To act in a deceptive, unethical way.
One used car salesperson in particular was well-known for playing fast and loose in his business practices.

play for keeps
To act with firm resolve, as if for a final result.
She joked often about being a frustrated Olympian, but when it came to competitive swimming she played for keeps.

play games
To behave manipulatively, insincerely, or deceptively.
Let's quit playing games and get down to serious business.

play hard to get
To show resistance toward.
I don't know whether he sincerely does not want to accept this new position or is simply playing hard to get.

play it by ear
To make decisions intuitively or moment by moment.
Instead of planning our every move, let's play it by ear.

play one's cards right
To make the right choices, given one's options.
Rapid career advancement in the company is possible if you play your cards right.

play possum
To pretend to be dead, inactive, or nonthreatening.
The cat was playing possum as a way of luring the bird into its grasp.

play second fiddle
To take a subordinate position to.
Conrad resented playing second fiddle to anyone when it came to his knowledge of telecommunications.

play the devil's advocate
To purposely espouse the opposed sides of an issue.
Let me play the devil's advocate and give you another perspective on the issue.

play the field
To extend one's social or other contacts widely rather than making single or narrow commitments.
Many college graduates continue to play the field in their dating habits rather than settling down to marriage and family as their parents did.

play with fire
To do dangerous things.
Those who play with fire inevitably get burned, and deservedly so.

(not) playing with a full deck
Not in possession of all one's mental faculties; crazy.
The leader was ambitious and charismatic, but at the same time we all suspected he was not playing with a full deck.

plumb the depths
To search for underlying issues or aspects.
The psychologist attempted to plumb the depths of the young man's intense fear of elevators.

poker face
A neutral or ambiguous facial expression.
By maintaining a poker face, she took maximum advantage of her opponent's strategies.

polish the apple
To seek favor through a compliment or complimentary behavior.
Now that you are an accepted and valued member of the team, you don't have to polish the apple with the boss each day.

poor as a church mouse
Extremely impoverished.
One of the most intelligent people I have ever met was as poor as a church mouse.

poor-mouth
To represent oneself as more impoverished than one is.
His obvious attempts to poor-mouth his situation left even his best friends unsympathetic.

pop the question
To make a sudden (usually important) inquiry, as in a marriage proposal.
Should he pop the question or should she?

(the) pot calling the kettle black
As if ignorant of its own faults, one party accusing another party of flaws or guilt.
A criminal who calls the police unnecessarily violent is often demonstrating a case of the pot calling the kettle black.

pound of flesh
Harsh terms demanded for revenge.
*He backed away from open conflict for now, but he will no
doubt return to demand his pound of flesh.*

pound the pavement
To work tediously by going door to door, or other
labor involving walking on city streets.
*The marketing surveyors did not know their work would
involve pounding the pavement so much.*

power behind the throne
The real authority or strength behind the ostensible
leader.
*History is full of examples of little-known men and women
who were, in fact, the power behind the throne.*

power broker
One who acts as an intermediary and negotiator
between influential parties.
*She served for years as power broker to the rich, famous,
and influential.*

press the flesh
To shake hands, often in a routine way.
*The candidate was confident that he could win votes by
pressing the flesh at malls and food stores.*

pretty kettle of fish
A sarcastic expression for a problem or dilemma.
*The woman stared at her uprooted plants and exclaimed,
"This is a pretty kettle of fish!"*

proof of the pudding is in the eating
Experiencing something makes its value clear.
*Don't make a long-term commitment to a career until you
have tried it for a few months; the proof of the pudding is
in the eating.*

pull one's punches
To purposely withhold some of the impact of one's influence or action.

At the meeting he didn't pull any punches; we knew exactly what he wanted and why.

pull out all the stops
To withhold nothing in one's efforts.

To finish the project on time, every team member pulled out all the stops.

pull out of a hat
To produce by surprise, as if by magic.

Somehow, the troubled couple expected the counselor to pull the answer out of a hat.

pull someone's leg
Tease someone.

Are you sure his comments were not just an awkward attempt to pull your leg?

pull something off
To make something happen, often against unfavorable odds.

I'm confident that we can pull this plan off if we all give it our best effort.

pull the plug on
To terminate.

Reluctantly, everyone had to admit that it was time to pull the plug on the plan to double the size of the state park.

pull the rug out from under
To cause a sudden reversal or collapse by changing underlying rules or assumptions.

She expressed shock and dismay when her supervisor pulled the rug out from under her plan.

pull the wool over one's eyes
To deceive.
You may be able to pull the wool over some people's eyes, but you haven't fooled me.

pull yourself up by your bootstraps
To improve oneself or one's situation by one's own means.
It's a confidence-building experience to pull yourself up by your own bootstraps at least once in life.

punch the clock
To show up at work, with the implication of punctuality and routinization.
She was tired of working and didn't want to punch the clock anymore.

pure gravy
Unalloyed profit or benefit.
After the restaurant was paid off, everything they made after taxes was pure gravy.

push one's buttons
To arouse someone's emotions, especially anger.
An experienced manager doesn't let others push his or her buttons.

push the envelope
To approach, test, or extend the limits.
The test pilot pushed the envelope in testing the new jet.

put a Band-Aid on
To repair in a temporary way.
The legislation merely put a Band-Aid on the problem of illegal immigration.

put all one's eggs in one basket
To invest in or rely upon only one source for one's security or benefit.
The investment advisor counseled the couple to diversify and to not put all their eggs in one basket.

put on airs
To presume an elevated status.
It was refreshing to see an actor who put on no airs in accepting his Oscar.

put on the dog
To dress or behave pretentiously.
She surprised her friends and gratified her enemies by putting on the dog.

put on the map
To make visible or create notice or reputation for.
His fame put his tiny hometown on the map.

put one's two cents in
To give one's opinion or advice.
When Grandfather asked for advice, everyone in the family put his or her two cents in.

put out fires
To resolve problems.
The elementary school principal spent half her day putting out fires of one kind or another.

put up or shut up
To act or stop talking about action.
Now that all aspects of the deal have been defined, it's time to put up or shut up.

put on your thinking cap
To begin intense mental work, as in problem-solving.
To consider the problem in a new way, put on your thinking cap and wait for inspiration.

Q

quantum leap

Significant progress.

> *The invention led to a quantum leap for the space program.*

quick and dirty

Something done rapidly and without attention to quality.

> *His sketch for the renovation was quick and dirty, but it sufficed to communicate our basic ideas to the architect.*

quick study

Fast learner.

> *After watching Jack master mah-jongg in one evening, we all realized he was a quick study.*

quit while one is ahead

To stop at a point of progress beyond the average or breakeven point.

> *One lesson never taught in school is how to quit while one is ahead.*

R

rain on one's parade

To bring negative influence, information, or events to one's otherwise positive experience.

You have every right to complain about your own problems, but please don't rain on my parade.

raining cats and dogs

Raining heavily.

The weather forecaster said it would be stormy and raining cats and dogs by sundown.

rainy day

A time of misfortune or a time when things are bad.

We tried to save a bit each month for a rainy day.

raise Cain

To cause problems or uproar.

The neighbors raised Cain when a carpenter began constructing a fence along their property line.

raise eyebrows

To cause surprise, particularly of a negative kind.

Susan's harsh words about the mayor raised eyebrows at the party.

raise the roof

To cause an uproar.

The guests at the graduation party raised the roof from midnight to the crack of dawn.

rats deserting a sinking ship

Early indications of coming destruction.

The rash of sudden resignations reminded us of rats deserting a sinking ship.

raw deal

Unwelcome or undeserved result.

Larry received a raw deal in being forced to retire two years before his pension came due.

read one like a book

To perceive a person's thoughts or motives.

After many years together, the couple could read one another like a book, even without saying a word.

read the riot act

To rebuke strongly or give stern admonition to.

The manager had to read the riot act to employees who insisted on taking two-hour lunches.

red as a beet

Flushed, usually with embarrassment or anger.

After losing the game, the coach was red as a beet with frustration and anger.

red herring

A false issue introduced to obscure the real issue.

The issue of seat belts in school buses is a red herring in the larger debate over the regulation of public transportation of children.

red in the face

Flushed, usually with anger or embarrassment.

She was red in the face with embarrassment after calling her new boyfriend by her old boyfriend's name.

red-letter day

A special occasion.

The date of his safe return from Vietnam remained a red-letter day for John throughout his life.

rest assured

To be confident.

Rest assured that your life insurance will provide adequate funds for the needs of your survivors.

ride roughshod over

Treat impolitely or without regard for feelings.

The boss had a bad habit of riding roughshod over the feelings and ideas of his subordinates.

right as rain
True; unwavering.
> *In morality and character, Richard was right as rain.*

(the) right hand doesn't know what the left hand is doing
One entity acts without knowing the related actions of another entity.
> *Especially in the executive branch, the right hand doesn't seem to know what the left hand is doing.*

ring a bell
Be familiar to; remind one of something.
> *Laura wrote that she had told me about her new book, but that didn't ring any bells.*

(a) roadmap to (for)
A guide or unmistakable information for.
> *The Internet information was a virtual roadmap for creating various types of bombs.*

rob Peter to pay Paul
To take money or other benefit away from one party to give it to another party.
> *Taking money from education to give to crime prevention is robbing Peter to pay Paul.*

rock bottom
Nadir; absolute lowest point.
> *Henry's personal life hit rock bottom after his divorce, job termination, and serious illness.*

(don't) rock the boat
Don't disturb the existing order.
> *If things are going smoothly in your career, don't rock the boat.*

(not a) rocket scientist
An extraordinarily bright person, often used sarcastically.
> *Robert's oldest son was not a rocket scientist, but he graduated with high marks due to his hard work.*

rocky start
A problem-plagued beginning.
Their relationship got off to a rocky start, especially during Evan's three-month absence for military service.

roll out the red carpet
To provide special treatment.
The whole community rolled out the red carpet for its returning Olympic medalist.

rotten apple
A person of poor character.
The morale of an entire workplace can be dragged down by the attitudes and actions of one rotten apple.

rotten to the core
Flawed or spoiled, not merely at the surface, but throughout.
Although he liked to find good in everyone, Frank had to admit that Ricky seemed rotten to the core.

rough someone up
To physically assault someone, but not to the point of inflicting life-threatening injuries.
The days are long past when a loan shark could physically rough someone up for not paying on time.

rub salt into one's wounds
To make a bad situation or hurt feelings even worse.
Being criticized by her own parents for her marital problems rubbed salt into Linda's wounds.

rub the wrong way
To treat in an unwelcome or uncomfortable manner, or to perceive such treatment.
The way he gives orders without listening to my ideas rubs me the wrong way.

(the) rubber meets the road
The point at which theoretical or untested matters
become tested by reality.
*When foreign officers arrive at their posts for the first time,
the rubber meets the road as far as diplomacy is concerned.*

rubberneck
To gawk.
*Dozens of cars slowed on the freeway as drivers rubber-
necked to look at the accident.*

ruffled feathers
Negative feelings, but not to an extreme degree.
*His comments initially caused ruffled feathers, which were
quickly smoothed by an apology.*

rugged individualist
A loner; independent thinker, with the implication
of physical or intellectual strength.
*Erik is a rugged individualist who claims to depend
on no one and nothing but himself in difficult
situations.*

run for one's money
A significant level of competition.
*Barbara will give you a run for your money on the tennis
court.*

run-in
An encounter, usually negative in implication.
*After his run-in with the law, Thomas vowed to keep better
company.*

run-of-the-mill
Usual; average.
*The quality of his work was run-of-the-mill, but its quantity
was prodigious.*

run on empty

To continue to function, but at the end of one's supply of energy; be near depletion.

Weeks after the trying ordeal, he still felt he was running on empty inside.

run (it) past (you)

To give one a cursory view or summary.

Let me run the idea past you before sending it on to the executive committee.

run the gamut

To extend across the entire range.

Our product line runs the gamut from sportswear to dress shoes.

S

saber rattling

Threats of hostile action.

The president warned that saber rattling would not change the course of international events.

(on the) same page

Similar or compatible mindsets, assumptions, or perception of information.

Fortunately, the entire collaborative writing team was on the same page when it came to their sense of purpose.

save for a rainy day

To set aside for use at a time of misfortune or reduced means.

By putting aside some money each month, the couple was able to save for a rainy day.

scrape the bottom of the barrel

To select the least attractive options.

In hiring the inexperienced young man, the company seems to be scraping the bottom of the barrel.

scratch one's back

To perform a gratifying service in expectation of similar service in return.

Among the workers, a system of favors had developed in which one group scratched another group's backs.

scratch the surface

To deal with insignificant or elementary aspects.

Scientists have just begun to scratch the surface of human genome research.

seat of the pants

Intuitive or moment-by-moment judgments, usually with negative implication.

Our last leader made decisions by the seat of the pants rather than by dialogue.

seeing is believing
Witnessing something convinces one of its truth.
We all doubted that a fish could grow so large, but seeing is believing.

seeing pink elephants
Hallucinating, as during or after inebriation.
Jason had been seeing pink elephants for weeks before seeking professional help.

sell one a bill of goods
To deceive.
She felt her son had been sold a bill of goods by the greedy clerk.

selling like hotcakes
Selling quickly.
Compact discs were selling like hotcakes compared to tapes.

send someone from pillar to post
To dispatch someone from place to place, with the implication of frustration resulting.
It makes little sense to send someone from pillar to post rather than giving clear directions in the first place.

separate the men from the boys
To distinguish the most able from the least able.
The rope climb separates the men from the boys in basic physical training.

separate the sheep from the goats
To distinguish the desirable from the undesirable.
One way to separate the sheep from the goats is to pose a moral dilemma and ask how each would respond.

set one's heart on
To yearn for; look forward earnestly to.
The things you set your heart on as a teenager are rarely the same things you yearn for as an adult.

set one's house in order
To arrange one's affairs (financial, organizational, personal).
>   *Prior to his trip abroad, Ben worked diligently to set his house in order in case he didn't return.*

set one's teeth on edge
To irritate one; grate upon.
>   *The static from the transmission set my teeth on edge.*

shaky ground
Weak evidence or support.
>   *You're on shaky ground when you use medical information direct from the Internet without checking it out with a physician or other medical professional.*

shape up or ship out
To reform one's behavior or leave.
>   *The director told the movie crew to shape up or ship out.*

(one's) ship comes in
Good fortune (often financial) arrives.
>   *Living in expectation of one's ship coming in can lead to frustration and missed opportunities.*

shoe on the other foot
A problem or circumstance associated with one person or side of an issue that becomes associated with another (usually opposed) person or side of an issue.
>   *Paul enjoyed working as a carpenter on other peoples' houses, but now that he owns his own house, the shoe is on the other foot.*

shoot fish in a barrel
To take advantage of an easy opportunity.
>   *Selling laptop computers to college students was like shooting fish in a barrel.*

shoot from the hip

To act or speak impulsively, without forethought.

We admired and feared Malcolm's habit of shooting from the hip when confronted by reporters.

shoot oneself in the foot

To act in a way that is detrimental to one's own interests.

No matter how much training we provided for the CEO, he continued to shoot himself in the foot during virtually every media interview he participated in.

shoot the breeze

To chat informally.

Come in, relax, and shoot the breeze with me for a while.

short and sweet

Concise and easy.

Her report was effective because it was short and sweet.

short end of the stick

The least desirable aspect of an action.

Ned got the short end of the stick when the company transferred him to Alaska instead of Hawaii.

short fuse

A quick temper.

His short fuse was legendary in the company, especially among those who had been the objects of his temper.

short straw

Least lucky; a sign that one must accept duties that others have escaped by better luck.

George drew the short straw and got stuck paying for every-one's meal.

(in) short supply

Scarce.

Loyal workers are in short supply.

(a) shot in the arm
A boost; motivator.

The lowering of interest rates gave a shot in the arm to company stock prices.

shouting match
A heated verbal exchange.

Our senior managers have an unspoken agreement not to participate in shouting matches with one another.

showstopper
A highlight, with the implication of avid approval from an audience.

Wendy's multimedia presentation at the convention was a showstopper.

shred of evidence
A bit of supporting information.

The district attorney brought the case forward even though she did not have a shred of evidence.

sigh of relief
An actual or metaphorical release of tension.

With a collective sigh of relief, the company directors signed the release of liability document ending the lawsuit.

silence is golden
Quiet is highly valued.

In those quiet moments after the children have fallen asleep, silence is golden.

silver lining
Unanticipated good in an otherwise bad situation.

She believed that even the darkest clouds seem to have some kind of silver lining.

sink or swim
To either survive or accept destruction.

In evaluating the takeover offer, we faced the option of whether to sink or swim as a company.

sit on the fence
To be undecided.
> *The entire community wished that the neighborhood association would quit* sitting on the fence *in an effort to please everyone.*

sit tight
To take no action.
> *There are times when no action is the right action and it's better simply to* sit tight.

sitting pretty
In an attractive or advantageous position.
> *We should be* sitting pretty *after receiving our share of the insurance settlement.*

six feet under
Buried; said of human burial.
> *The gunslinger was eventually buried* six feet under *in Tombstone, Arizona.*

six of one, half dozen of the other
One option is comparable to another.
> *Whether to fly or take the train doesn't matter for such a short distance; it's* six of one, half dozen of the other.

skate on thin ice
To endanger; act in reliance upon support that, in fact, cannot be trusted.
> *In trusting your legal records to an uninsured bank, you're* skating on thin ice.

skeleton in one's closet
Negative personal information that one hides.
> *There's probably at least one* skeleton in everyone's closet *if they look hard enough.*

(by the) skin of one's teeth
Barely.
> *Our runners qualified for the race* by the skin of their teeth.

(no) skin off one's nose
(No) injury or ill effect.
> *Even though the problem may seem serious to you, it's no skin off my nose.*

skyrocketing costs
Rapidly rising expenses.
> *Skyrocketing costs for gasoline caused us to postpone our trip by car across the United States.*

(the) sky's the limit
Boundless; limitless.
> *The sky's the limit when it comes to buying equipment for the sailboat.*

slam dunk
Strong, quick action that proves successful.
> *After receiving high test scores, Sam found that admission to the college of his choice was a slam dunk.*

slip of the tongue
Unintentional verbal mistake.
> *His slip of the tongue caused both embarrassment and financial loss.*

slip through the cracks
To not be attended to because of flaws in the usual system.
> *Too many of our orders have been slipping through the cracks at the supply warehouse.*

slow as molasses
Excruciatingly slow.
> *The pace of the meeting seemed slow as molasses to Alvin.*

small potatoes
Trivial matters; little money.
> *Working for small potatoes at her day job meant that Ellen had to find additional work in the evenings.*

small talk
Inconsequential chatter
The interviewer made small talk for the first five minutes of the interview.

smell a rat
To perceive the first signs of a problem.
The auditor reviewed the financial records with care and eventually smelled a rat.

smell the roses
To enjoy life.
Hard work means little unless one also takes time to smell the roses.

smoke and mirrors
Trickery.
The senator's charismatic effect on audiences was largely a matter of smoke and mirrors.

smoke screen
An intentional barrier set up to prevent enlightenment or discovery.
The board of review found it difficult to sort fact from fiction due to the smoke screen of alibis and excuses put forward by the defendant.

smoking gun
Undeniable evidence of one's involvement, with negative implications.
The auditors found evidence that there was something irregular in the records but could not locate a smoking gun to tie Kelly to any crime.

snowball's chance in hell
No possibility.
We have no better than a snowball's chance in hell of finding affordable tickets to the homecoming game.

solid ground
Firm, well-supported basis.

You're on solid ground when you base your argument on widely agreed-upon statistics.

something fishy
Something amiss or suspicious.

In spite of appearances, we felt there was something fishy about Frieda's sudden departure.

something rotten in Denmark
Something wrong.

Her hurried handwritten note convinced us that something was rotten in Denmark.

song and dance
An activity that does not relate to or attempts to obscure the real issue.

After the introductory song and dance about product benefits, the sales manager began to discuss real applications and product problems.

sound off
To express oneself assertively, often with emotion.

We all valued our right to sound off whenever necessary to prevent the company from making serious mistakes.

sounding board
An audience on which to test a concept, proposal, or other idea.

Two consultants served as sounding boards for the ideas put forward by our Advanced Design unit.

sour grapes
Bitter feelings or actions based on feelings experienced by one who does not win in a competition or faces another misfortune.

His angry complaints after the bowling tournament were nothing more than sour grapes.

sow one's wild oats
To act recklessly, especially in one's youth.
Sowing one's wild oats does not mean hurting others for the sake of thrills.

speak of the devil
Said when a person appears just after being referred to in conversation.
We were talking about Fred and, speak of the devil, he walked into the room.

speak volumes
To reveal much about.
Your care with your garden speaks volumes about your character.

speak with a forked tongue
To present contradictory and intentionally deceptive messages.
Some parents felt the principal spoke with a forked tongue in trying to appease both the community and the teachers' union.

spin doctor
One who attempts to influence how information will be perceived.
The administration called in a well-known spin doctor to help control damage and manage public perception.

split hairs
To quibble.
I don't mind discussing the issue, but let's not waste time splitting hairs.

spread like wildfire
To extend range and influence very quickly.
The illness spread like wildfire across three continents.

spread oneself too thin
To have too many commitments.
It's tempting to spread oneself too thin in an effort to please as many people as possible.

squeaky wheel gets the grease
The one who complains the loudest gets the most attention.
The quick response James got to his terse memo proves that the squeaky wheel gets the grease.

stamping ground
Home or native region.
It felt strange to return to her stamping ground after three decades of absence.

stand on ceremony
To maintain formalities.
Please don't stand on ceremony; we appreciate informal conversation here.

state-of-the-art
The latest form of development.
You are entering a state-of-the-art biosphere protected entirely from the outside atmosphere.

steal one's thunder
To act in such a way that another person's subsequent action becomes anticlimactic.
Lydia accidentally stole her boss's thunder by mentioning that the General Motors contract had just been signed.

steer clear
To avoid.
Steer clear of situations that may later be interpreted as sexual harassment.

stem to stern
Entire; end-to-end.
>*The entire organization needed an overhaul, from stem to stern.*

step on it
To hurry.
>*Our flight leaves in half an hour and we need to step on it.*

stick in one's craw
To be unacceptable, irritating to embrace.
>*Wasting tax money on programs that don't work continues to stick in my craw.*

stick out like a sore thumb
To be obvious to all observers.
>*That hat is going to stick out like a sore thumb at the party.*

stick to one's guns
To maintain one's purpose, commitment.
>*Walter knew how to stick to his guns without making others feel bullied.*

sticking point
A controversial issue; difficult item for negotiation.
>*Only one sticking point remained in the contract: the non-competition clause for employees who quit the company.*

stir up a hornet's nest
To cause angry reactions.
>*The columnist's assertions stirred up a hornet's nest at the mayor's office.*

stone sober
Not under the influence of any substance.
>*He appeared stone sober at his arraignment for drunk driving.*

straight and narrow
Strict; rigid; unwavering.

Following the straight and narrow *may be safe but it also proves boring at times.*

straight from the horse's mouth
Direct from the source.

We trust the story because it came straight from the horse's mouth.

straighten matters out
To clarify; resolve; make peace through mutual understanding.

If you will give me just ten minutes of your time, I'm sure I can straighten matters out *to your satisfaction.*

straw in the wind
A small but significant indicator of future trends.

The downturn in high-tech stocks was a straw in the wind *for the direction of the entire stock market.*

straw man
A stand-in created to draw attention or argument away from the central issue.

John's remarks about sabotage of company equipment proved to be a straw man *that kept us from seeing the larger problem.*

straw that breaks the camel's back
The final detail or aspect that causes a larger development to fall apart.

The budget item for chocolate bars proved to be the straw that broke the camel's back *and exhausted the patience of the school board.*

strike while the iron is hot
To act while circumstances are propitious.

Most advertising agencies recommend that their clients strike while the iron is hot *in the marketplace.*

string someone along
To continue to entice someone's involvement by
deceptive representations.
*We usually resent it when someone we trust strings us
along for personal gain.*

strings attached
Other unspecified obligations or entanglements associated with a transaction.
*This deal comes with significant strings attached,
including government review and reapproval
each year.*

strong, silent type
A quiet, self-assured person, with implications
of physical strength or strength of character.
*Ernest thought of himself as the strong, silent type,
although others perceived him as sullen and arrogant.*

stuff the ballot box
To unethically influence a vote toward one's favor.
*She got herself elected only by a concerted effort to stuff the
ballot box.*

sugar daddy
A male, usually older, who obtains affection from
others through material gifts and lavish spending.
*The drama students sought a sugar daddy to fund the pro-
duction of their play.*

swallow hook, line, and sinker
To accept completely, often with deceptive intentions
implied.
*Against my better judgment, I swallowed his representa-
tions hook, line, and sinker.*

sweeten the pot
To make a deal or offer more attractive.
> *Before we can recommend this deal to our client, you must sweeten the pot by at least ten percent.*

sweet tooth
An affection for sweets.
> *Dentists meet many people who have a sweet tooth.*

(don't) switch horses in midstream
(Don't) Change leadership at times of stress or crisis.
> *The president's slogan for reelection was "Don't switch horses in midstream."*

T

tail between one's legs
A sign of cowardice or fearfulness.
After all his prior boasting, Fred left the chess match with his tail between his legs.

take a bath
To experience extraordinary financial loss or other misfortune.
Some investors take a bath in the stock market, then sell before their stocks rebound in value.

take a gander
To look at in a spontaneous, casual way.
If you want to see an example of superb vegetable gardening, take a gander over my fence.

take a page from someone's book
To borrow ideas from another.
We should consider taking a page from our competitor's book instead of trying to come up with an original approach to the market.

take a rain check
To arrange for the same or similar opportunity at a later date.
May we take a rain check for a time when we don't face time conflicts?

take by storm
To influence or capture in a sudden way.
The opera diva took New York by storm.

take for a ride
To deceive through diversion.
It was obvious that we were being taken for a ride by the con man, but I must say that the ride was enjoyable.

take heart

To become confident, hopeful.

Especially at times of discouragement, you can take heart in the knowledge that you have friends who care about you.

take it from the top

To begin at the beginning.

We're not getting anywhere in our discussions, so let's take it from the top.

take it on the chin

To receive a negative impact in a way that threatens one's stability or survival.

The director of marketing admitted that the company took it on the chin from the competition last quarter.

take one to task

To blame one for poor performance; admonish.

The coach had to take the player to task for poor study habits.

take pains to

To be diligent through intense attention.

We wanted to take pains to appear customer-friendly.

take stock

To evaluate.

By taking stock of our current situation, we can prepare a plan for the coming fiscal year.

take the bull by the horns

To engage a problem directly and forcefully.

Above all, the company needed a leader who could take the bull by the horns.

take the fall

To accept the blame and consequences.

After his brief stay in prison, Jake was sure he would be singled out to take the fall for other crimes committed in his neighborhood.

take the fifth
To refuse to divulge information, especially information that may prove self-incriminating.
The secretary did not need a lawyer's advice in deciding to take the fifth regarding any knowledge of the boss's private life.

take the plunge
To take action that, once begun, cannot be reversed.
There are times in life when one has to take the plunge rather than remain a spectator.

take the wind out of one's sails
To remove the motivation, confidence, or energy from one's actions.
The announcement of currency devaluations in Asia, our major market, took the wind out of our sails and sent our stock plummeting.

take to the cleaners
To experience severe financial or other losses, with deception implied.
Clearly, he had been taken to the cleaners by professional con artists.

take under one's wing
To care for in a maternal way.
Martha's kind spirit motivated her to take the youngster under her wing.

take up the cudgels
To prepare for hostile engagement.
It's time to quit talking and to take up the cudgels to settle this matter once and for all.

take with a grain of salt
To consider skeptically.
Venture capital firms are adept at taking the claims of inventors and entrepreneurs with a grain of salt.

talk in circles
To speak in a repetitive way that leads to no conclusion.
*He could talk in circles for hours without saying anything,
but also without boring his audience.*

talk through one's hat
To speak without knowing what one is talking about.
*When you begin to predict weather patterns a year in
advance, it's obvious you're talking through your hat.*

talk turkey
To speak frankly or bluntly, usually about beneficial
matters.
*Give us a call when you have checked with your boss and
are ready to talk turkey.*

tall in the saddle
Positioned like a leader or hero.
*The company executive rode tall in the saddle for his first
six months on the job.*

tall order
Large and challenging expectation.
*You're presenting us with a tall order, but I'm sure we can
meet the challenge.*

team player
One who is adept at interacting with others in an
activity.
*A team player pays attention not only to what others on
the team are doing but also to what they are thinking
and feeling.*

tell it like it is
To reveal the truth in a plain, honest way.
*Don't rehearse your testimony too thoroughly; simply tell it
like it is.*

there's the rub
Describing the point at which controversy, disagreement, or discomfort arises.

He is related to the boss by marriage, and there's the rub; he cannot be sure his rapid promotion is due solely to his merit.

thick as thieves
With bonds of loyalty and collusion characteristic of thieves.

The governor and his construction industry cronies were as thick as thieves around election time.

think outside the box
To imagine or consider aspects outside the usual frame of reference.

Learning to break the rules occasionally is a prerequisite for thinking outside the box.

thirty pieces of silver
Ill-gotten financial gain from despicable acts.

The business broker received his thirty pieces of silver for negotiating the hostile takeover of our company.

three-ring circus
An environment characterized by several types of energetic activity.

On any given day, their home is a three-ring circus of domestic and social activity.

throw a curve
To present or deliver a deceptive, unexpected, or difficult-to-handle idea or action.

Your last set of ideas threw me a curve; please explain them in detail.

throw a wet blanket on
To downplay; show no enthusiasm for.

We don't want to throw a wet blanket on your plans, but there simply is no budget to fund them.

throw caution to the wind

To act recklessly.

For his fiftieth birthday, Winston threw caution to the wind and took up rollerblading.

throw down the gauntlet

To issue a challenge.

There was excitement in working for a company that did not hesitate to throw down the gauntlet to larger competitors.

throw in the towel

To give up; surrender.

The team refused to throw in the towel even when they lagged behind by more than a dozen points on the scoreboard.

throw money at something

To attempt to solve a problem by spending large sums of money on it.

The solution clearly does not lie in simply throwing money at the problem.

throw off the scent

To act to deceive a pursuer.

His faked memos and E-mail messages were composed in an effort to throw investigators off the scent.

throw one's hat in the ring

To enter a competition.

There is no time like the present to throw one's hat in the ring and run for office.

throw one's weight around

To use one's influence aggressively or ostentatiously.

The mayor enjoys throwing his weight around in his own city.

throw the book at

To give the maximum allowable punishment to.

The judge vowed to throw the book at the reckless driver if he was arrested again.

thumbnail sketch

A quick, approximate representation.

Let me give you a thumbnail sketch of our plans and we can fill in the details later.

tie one on

To become drunk.

Conrad foolishly decided to tie one on a few hours before his presentation to the executive committee.

tighten one's belt

To commit to making do with fewer resources.

Smaller budgets mean that we will all have to tighten our belts and make resources stretch as far as possible.

tilt at windmills

To take on unnecessary and foolish challenges.

Do you find pleasure in tilting at windmills, or do you really believe you are pursuing a worthwhile activity?

tip of the iceberg

The slight visible portion of a much larger problem, issue, or other matter.

The threat of food poisoning is just the tip of the iceberg when it comes to owning a chain of restaurants.

tip the scales

To weigh in.

The huge wrestler tipped the scales at more than 350 pounds.

to the bitter end

To the end, even when suffering and disappointment are involved.

We resolved to remain loyal to one another to the bitter end.

to the hilt

To the maximum degree.

The newlyweds decided to take a cruise and they enjoyed it to the hilt.

toe the line
To remain in strict compliance with rules or standards.
New employees often feel undue pressure to toe the line, even when they are not sure where the line is.

tongue in cheek
With ironic or teasing intent.
She spoke tongue in cheek, although her words were taken literally by some.

too big for one's britches
Too egotistical for one's true position and abilities.
One student in particular is getting too big for his britches and needs talking to.

too hot to handle
Too hazardous or involved with potential problems.
This issue is too hot to handle without the involvement of attorneys.

top banana
The person in charge; most important person.
Jack has been top banana at that company for more than ten years.

top drawer
High quality or high importance.
We all considered her contribution top drawer and told the boss so.

top flight
Best; most skilled.
Finding a top-flight mechanic is much harder than finding an expensive car to purchase.

topsy-turvy
Confused; disordered; upside down.
The whole venture went topsy-turvy after Oliver's sudden resignation.

touch (tag) all the bases
To take care of all obligations in a process.
> *I know you're eager to complete the project, but let's take time to make sure we've touched all the bases first.*

touchy-feely
Characterized by subjective, emotional qualities as opposed to rational attributes.
> *Some of the training sessions were too touchy-feely to be useful in a practical way for the employees.*

tough act to follow
A performance so high in quality or approval that it intimidates subsequent performers.
> *Benson's long and distinguished career with the company will be a tough act to follow.*

tough sledding
Difficult progress.
> *There's probably tough sledding ahead for smaller colleges that cannot compete in scholarships and facilities with larger, richer schools.*

train wreck
A sudden disaster.
> *The unexpected resignation of the company director was considered a train wreck by the stockholders.*

tried-and-true
Proven successful through experience.
> *Young people tire of being told to practice tried-and-true techniques.*

trigger-happy
Too eager to release force.
> *Four of our clients are trigger-happy when it comes to suing competitors.*

trust him as far as you can throw him
Untrustworthy.
> *After his last display of ineptitude, I don't trust him as far as I can throw him.*

turn a deaf ear to
To fail to pay attention to; refuse to listen to.
> *Please don't turn a deaf ear to charities that invite and deserve your support.*

turn on a dime
To turn in a small radius.
> *The sports car will turn on a dime without losing traction.*

turn one's stomach
To cause a negative response comparable to nausea.
> *Some scenes in the movie are so violent that they almost turn one's stomach.*

turn over in one's grave
To respond with disapproval even though one cannot influence the offending course of action.
> *Our company founder would turn over in her grave if she could see the way the company is being run today.*

turn the other cheek
To forgive and overlook an insult or other offense.
> *I have an easier time turning the other cheek in personal relationships than in business.*

turn the tables
To reverse position or relative advantage.
> *We eventually found a way to turn the tables on our adversary.*

twist of fate
An odd, unaccountable occurrence.
> *By an odd twist of fate, he worked at the same desk his grandfather had used fifty years before.*

twist one's arm

To coerce.

> *The seller doesn't want to leave the piano with the house, but you may be able to twist his arm to do so.*

two-faced

Duplicitous; deceptive.

> *The once-trusted friend eventually proved to be two-faced.*

two peas in a pod

Virtually identical to one another and closely aligned.

> *Her two children nestled into bed together like two peas in a pod.*

two strikes against one

At a point at which past mistakes leave one few chances for success.

> *Her past mistakes count as two strikes against her; a third will probably mean her termination.*

U

under one's hat
To oneself; privately.
Please keep this sensitive information under your hat.

under one's nose
Obvious.
How could he ignore such actions happening right under his nose?

under one's thumb
Under close control, with negative implications.
Eventually she grew tired of trying to survive under his thumb.

under the sun
Everywhere.
We looked everywhere under the sun for those papers.

under the table
Not through accepted or legal channels.
Some of the profits were passed under the table instead of through normal channels.

under the weather
Ill, but not with life-threatening implications.
Our usual announcer is under the weather today.

under the wire
Just in time.
We handed in our work just under the wire.

under wraps
Held hidden; in secret.
It's extremely important that we keep details about the project under wraps.

until the cows come home
Until the last moment.
You can complain until the cows come home but it will not change the situation.

up and running

Functioning as intended.

Believe it or not, we have a prototype of the invention up and running.

up for grabs

Not under sole control; available to others.

The entire company will be up for grabs unless the employees decide to buy it.

up (or down) one's alley

Appropriate for one's special area of skill, interest, or expertise.

That topic is right up your alley and should be easy to write about.

up the creek without a paddle

In trouble without the means to extricate oneself.

When half the staff was laid off, the rest of us found ourselves up the creek without a paddle in our efforts to complete major projects.

up the wall

To an extreme degree of frustration.

His attitude drives me up the wall, especially on days when everyone has to pitch in to get the work done.

(not) up to snuff

(Not) Up to acceptable standards.

The physician's records were not up to snuff as far as the IRS was concerned.

upper crust

Elite.

He did not belong to the upper crust and did not aspire to.

upset the applecart

To disturb an activity or the existing order.

Going public with this information will certainly upset the applecart at the company.

W

waiting for the other shoe to drop
After one event has occurred, expecting a companion event to also occur.

Although there were many compliments directed toward us, we waited for the other shoe to drop.

wake up and smell the coffee
To become alert to obvious signals or sensations.

If you do not think our workforce has motivational problems, you should wake up and smell the coffee.

walk a tightrope
To pursue a dangerous course.

A good negotiator walks a tightrope between stubbornness and charm.

walk before you run
To take on elementary matters before taking on more advanced matters.

Our early failures were due in large part to our refusal to walk before we ran.

walk on eggshells
Behaving with uncomfortable attention to propriety or sensitivity.

Staying with her in-laws made Gwen feel that she was walking on eggshells all the time.

walk the plank
To be forced to take actions that will bring one's destruction.

No executive will willingly walk the plank in public view.

walls have ears
One may be overheard in unexpected ways.

Be careful what you say because the walls have ears around here.

wash one's hands of
To abandon; disassociate oneself from.
It's too late to wash our hands of our business associates; we have to help them reform their image.

water off a duck's back
Matters that have no effect, prove inconsequential, have no impact upon feelings.
Ellis had an amazing ability to let criticism roll off him like water off a duck's back.

watered-down
Weakened in strength or quality.
You've read only the watered-down version of the document.

(a) way with words
Verbally skillful.
We needed a public relations officer who had a way with words.

wear and tear
Damage brought about by normal use.
The renters were not responsible for normal wear and tear sustained by the apartment.

wear one's heart on one's sleeve
To show one's emotions openly.
Jack's gratitude was apparent; he wore his heart on his sleeve.

wear two hats
To be responsible for performing two functions.
Most of us in the company wear at least two hats.

wet behind the ears
Naive; not yet experienced.
The younger players seemed still wet behind the ears.

what goes around comes around
A person's negative actions toward others eventually
return to have a negative effect upon that person.
*I try to be careful what I say about others, because what
goes around comes around.*

wheel and deal
To negotiate and reach agreements quickly and with
little regard for ordinary standards.
*Be prepared to wheel and deal if you want to buy a used
car at the best price.*

when it counts
At the most important or crucial time.
*James isn't always a top performer but he seems to come
through when it counts.*

white elephant
An object one wishes to get rid of, but either will not
or cannot.
*He obtained the white elephant at a garage sale two years
ago and has not been able to get rid of it.*

whole ball of wax
Entirety.
We asked her to be responsible for the whole ball of wax.

whole nine yards
The entire amount or distance.
*On Dayle's fortieth birthday she wanted the party, the
presents, and the whole nine yards.*

wild-goose chase
An extensive, intense, but unproductive search.
*Investigators found themselves on a wild-goose chase
carefully engineered by the guilty parties.*

wild hair
A person or organizational component characterized by nonconformist or incompatible opinions, actions, or ideas.
The boss valued the wild hair in the company for unusual and challenging perspectives on problems.

win hands down
To succeed with ease.
Lewis felt he could win hands down in a fair competition.

window dressing
Visible attributes that give a partial and often overly positive impression.
The core issues took only a page to describe; all the rest was window dressing.

wish list
A collection of hoped-for items or occurrences.
The children left their Christmas wish list taped to the refrigerator for all to see.

witch-hunt
An attempt to impose false charges on an innocent party through character assassination.
The so-called inquiry was in fact a witch-hunt, with the guilty parties predetermined by management.

with one's eyes closed
Easily; without conscious effort.
Ted boasted he could find his way home through the woods with his eyes closed.

with one's eyes wide open
Aware of all implications.
We all went into the deal with our eyes wide open.

world on a string
A period of high spirits and good fortune and everything in one's favor.

In an enthusiastic mood, the youngsters felt they had the world on a string.

would not be seen dead
Would absolutely avoid.

He said he would not be seen dead with his former roommate.

wrapped up in oneself
Overly concerned with oneself.

Even her best friends could not tell her that she was too wrapped up in herself.

wrap something up
To finish.

Although he could have written much more, it was time to wrap up the project.

wrath of Khan
Extreme anger.

Employees felt the wrath of Khan from the boss whenever they forgot to punch their time cards.

written all over one's face
Communicated nonverbally by one's expression.

No matter what your words, the truth is written all over your face.

wrong side of the tracks
A less prestigious or socially acceptable neighborhood or background.

He came from the wrong side of the tracks, but never apologized for it.